» Simple Guides
SHINTO

» Simple Guides

SHINTO

Ian Reader

Published in Great Britain by
Simple Guides, an imprint of Bravo Ltd
59 Hutton Grove, London N12 8DS
www.kuperard.co.uk
Enquiries: office@kuperard.co.uk

First published 1998 by Global Books Ltd.
Reprinted 2001
This edition published 2007

ISBN 978 1 85733 433 3

British Library Cataloguing in Publication Data
A CIP catalogue entry for this book
is available from the British Library

Printed in the USA

Cover image: *Torii* (shrine gateway) in the Japanese Gardens,
Birmingham, Alabama. *istockphoto/Philip Dyer*
Drawings by Irene Sanderson

About the Author

IAN READER has been teaching and researching on the religions of Japan for many years. His PhD on Japanese Buddhism was gained at the University of Leeds in 1983, after which he and his wife Dorothy lived and worked in Japan for almost six years. Since 1989 he has been a member of the Scottish Centre for Japanese Studies at the University of Stirling, Scotland. He also spent a year as a Visiting Professor at the University of Hawaii in 1992–93. For three years from August 1995 he lived in Copenhagen, Denmark, where he was a Senior Research Fellow at the Nordic Institute of Asian Studies.

Amongst his books are *Religion in Contemporary Japan* (Macmillan, 1991); *Pilgrimage in Popular Culture* (edited with Tony Walter, Macmillan, 1993) and *A Poisonous Cocktail? Aum Shinrikyō's Path to Violence* (NIAS Books, Copenhagen 1996).

For Norman and Joan Taylor, my parents-in-law.

⊙ Contents

List of Illustrations

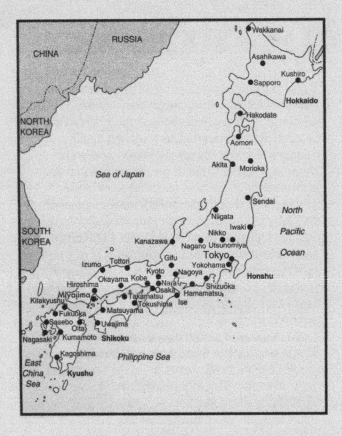

⊙ Map of Japan

The word 'Shinto' is a Japanese term which translates as 'the way of the gods', and refers to a religious tradition associated with the land and people of Japan. Shinto is a prominent element in that country's religious and physical landscape, with Shinto shrines being highly visible, whether in the main cities or in the mountains and countryside.

Japanese shops and small family businesses also may have their own shrines for the gods of business prosperity, as may Japanese factories and modern commercial enterprises as well. Japanese houses, too, may contain Shinto symbols of worship in the form of the *kamidana*, or Shinto household altar, that enshrines the household's protective deities.

The deities of Shinto may be called into action on many occasions throughout life, from life-cycle rituals to calendrical events, from the blessings given to newly-born babies at Shinto shrines – a form of first entry into society – to annual community festivals and celebratory events.

Shinto also expresses, through its myths and legends, various teachings and meanings concerned with issues of purity and correct behaviour, with attitudes to life and death, with the relationship between humans and deities, with the nature of the world, and of the life-forces that, according to Shinto, permeate it in the form of its gods, and with the roles and responsibilites of those gods in this world.

Shinto myths also assert that a special relationship exists between the people and landscape of Japan and the deities of Shinto, who serve as guardians and protectors of the country. This concept was expressed nowhere more famously than in the late thirteenth century, when Japan was threatened by invasion from the Mongol forces that had occupied China and were preparing a military assault on Japan, first in 1274 and then again in 1281. The Japanese Imperial court called for prayers to be said throughout the country, to seek divine protection against this threat.

When the ships bearing the invading Mongol armies were destroyed as a result of bad weather – thereby averting the only major threat to Japan's sovereignty until it was occupied by Allied forces after its defeat in 1945 – it was believed that the prayers of the nation had been answered by the gods, who had thus sent 'divine winds' – the literal meaning of the Japanese word *kamikaze* – for this purpose.

Mention of the term *kamikaze* conjures up darker images as well, alluding to Shinto's controversial association with Japanese nationalism and the role it played in the earlier part of the twentieth century in supporting the Imperial Japanese state during its period of militant expansion and war. It was in the name of the Emperor – depicted in pre-war Japan as a Shinto deity, a depiction based in Shinto myths of Imperial descent from the gods – that the *kamikaze* pilots flew their missions, and it was through the medium of Shinto that the Emperor was transformed into a figure of veneration in whose name wars were fought and the enemies of the state were suppressed.

This use of Shinto as a religion of state associated with the suppression of religious freedoms, and of aggressive nationalism, was a factor leading to the imposition on Japan of the post-war Constitution which separates religion and state and prohibits state support of religion – an issue which itself is a source of lingering controversy in the present day.

All these issues will be dealt with in this book, the aim of which is to explain what the religious tradition of Shinto means in terms of Japanese history and contemporary society, and to describe its meanings and myths, the teachings these embody, and the practices, rituals and festivals of Shinto. The earlier chapters will discuss what is meant by the term 'Shinto', and give an outline of its history, placing it within the broader context of Japanese religion. Shinto is, however, as has been noted above, a very visible presence in Japan which will be discussed later in the book when we consider Shinto in the present day, outlining the sorts of practices, rituals and festivals that visitors are likely to see if they go to Shinto shrines.

Thus, we will discover what Shinto shrines look like, what one is liable to see going on there, and what the various objects such as amulets and lucky charms that are sold at shrines mean, and why Japanese people purchase them. It will also introduce some important Shinto shrines and will draw attention to the visual spectacle and the publicly viewed phenomena of Shinto, from its wild and colourful festivals to its sedate rituals. However, just as the controversies associated with Shinto remain an ever-present element in the contemporary Japanese religious world so, too, will they be discussed here as well, with a chapter examining the problematic relationship of Shinto and the state and the issues this involves in the present day.

The materials on which I draw for this book range from historical documents and the academic writings of other scholars, to my own observations at countless Shinto shrines, festivals and ritual events over the past seventeen years since I first visited Japan in 1981. For a number of years in the 1980s my wife Dorothy and I lived and taught there, and during that period we visited many Shinto shrines, talked to Shinto priests, shrine maidens and practitioners, from the casual visitors to Shinto festivals, to those who visit their local shrines regularly to pray to the gods.

To all these anonymous people, and especially to the many Shinto priests who kindly responded to hours of my often tiresome questions, and who explained rituals and provided me with materials about them, I owe a debt of thanks. Academic colleagues have also aided me through their writings and through answers to questions, and here let me especially thank Karen Smyers of Wesleyan College, USA, whose work on Inari (probably the most widely venerated deity at Shinto shrines) has been extremely valuable and informative, and also Jay Sakashita who was most helpful with information on Shinto in Hawaii.

I owe an immense debt of thanks to my family for providing the sort of emotionally supportive atmosphere in which one can write books. I give many thanks to Dorothy, my wife, for her support over the years and for her help in asking the questions that produced the results found here. I also thank my children, Rosie, aged 9, and Philip, who is 6, who are not quite sure what I do for a living, except that they know I write books of some sort (although ones without the pictures and adventure stories that they would like), but who tolerate me nonetheless and give me loving strength.

My other debt is to my first publisher Paul Norbury, who conceived the idea of this series, inveigled me into cooperating in it, extracted an unwise and over-optimistic commitment from me to produce this book, made me feel guilty about not getting round to doing it and who finally, over a beer in Budapest, stirred my conscience so much that I promised a specific delivery date. Like all scholars I was late with this, and to Paul I owe an apology for the continuing indisciplines in my own life that have caused this to happen. Nonetheless, the book has materialized at last, and it thus serves as a testament to Paul's skilful use of persuasion. It is thanks to him that this short book – and the series in which it appears – has moved from being a figment of my, and his, imagination to a real event.

IAN READER
Copenhagen
April 1998

Wherever one goes in Japan one sees Shinto shrines, from the large and grandiose to tiny wayside structures, in such diverse locations as the roofs of department stores in the centres of large cities, and amidst rice fields deep in the countryside. The word 'shrine' is the word normally used in English for various Japanese terms such as *jinja*, *jingū* and *taisha* (the most common of these being *jinja*), all of which refer to Shinto religious institutions.

No one knows for sure how many such Shinto shrines there are in Japan, but conservative estimates run into several tens of thousands: the Japanese Ministry of Culture, which produces annual statistics on religion in Japan, cites a figure of over 90,000 Shinto establishments, but this does not include the numerous unmanned wayside shrines that dot Japan's highways, byways and mountain paths.

The single most widely venerated Shinto deity, Inari, popular as a deity of the rice harvest but widely respected in modern Japan as a god of business, is enshrined at over 30,000 shrines throughout the country, while other prominent

Shinto figures of worship such as Hachiman, a god of war, Amaterasu, traditionally venerated as the Sun Goddess and as an important figure in Japanese mythology, and Tenjin, the god of education and learning, all have many thousands of shrines dedicated to them. Besides such major and widely known deities (of whom those mentioned here are but a few) there are also countless other deities throughout Japan, some barely known outside their local environs, which also have shrines dedicated to them.

⊙ *Shinto shrine – offerings*

⊙ Torii – the Shinto gateway at Shiroyama shrine, Nagoya

❯❯ Terms for Shinto Shrines

jinja – general term meaning shrine (literally, shrine [*ja*] of the gods); *jin* is the same as *shin* or *kami*

yashiro – also a general term for a Shinto shrine, although normally used for small or sub-shrines

jingū – shrine, but usually referring to a major shrine, usually one that commands the respect and support of a lineage of shrines. The suffix *gū* means shrine, but also refers to shrines of some size and importance: thus we have the Ise Jingū and the Dazaifu Tenmangū shrines.

taisha – literally 'great shrine', refers also to major and important shrines, such as Izumo Taisha, Fushimi Inari Taisha.

Torii – the Shinto Gateway

The presence of such shrines is normally indicated by the *torii*, or Shinto shrine gateway. This comprises two slanting upright supports and cross-pieces usually painted vermillion. It is normally made out of wood but sometimes, especially in the present day, concrete. As all visitors know, it is one of the most common and most photogenic images of Japan. The *torii* of the Itsukushima shrine, for example, rising from the waters of the Inland Sea, is one of Japan's most famous and picturesque sights, gracing tourist guidebooks and photographic collections alike, and alluding to the close associations between Shinto, nature and the Japanese landscape.

While this association between Shinto and nature, hinted at in the presence of shrines in splendid natural settings, and affirmed by Shinto teachings about the vitality of nature, points to Shinto's deep-rooted associations with agriculture and especially with rural Japan (and, hence, with images of the traditional), this is only one element in its complex structure. Shinto shrines are not limited to the wilder parts of the country, nor to the beauties of its mountains and other such areas of natural splendour, nor to the tranquil rural environment. Indeed, they are also found in the heart of its modern cities, in the environmentally polluted wastelands of industrial Japan, and in places most commonly associated with the country's commercial prowess.

Atop the headquarters of one of Japan's major manufacturers of cosmetics, the Shiseidō company, in the Ginza in central Tokyo, for example, one finds a *torii* signifying the presence of a Shinto shrine, the Seidō Inari shrine, dedicated to the company's protective guardian deity Inari. Other rooftop shrines in the Ginza area also testify to the presence of the Shinto gods at the heart of Japan's commercial power. Even in the modern city and the modern industrial economy of Japan, the *torii* remains a constant symbol.

Meiji Jingū Shrine

Elsewhere in central Tokyo, a massive *torii* signals entry into the sacred grounds of one of the largest and most visited of all Shinto shrines, the Meiji

Jingū (shrine), which occupies spacious grounds in the heart of the city, surrounded by trees, and approached by a long path many metres wide. The shrine is named after the Emperor Meiji, who ascended the throne in 1868 and in whose name the upheaval known as the Meiji Restoration occurred, which swept away Japan's old feudal regime, moved the capital to Tokyo from Kyoto, and set in motion the process of modernization that produced the modern nation state of Japan.

After Meiji's death in 1912, a shrine was built in Tokyo to enshrine his spirit as a *kami:* this word, *kami*, which means deity or god in Japanese, is a crucial term and concept for understanding Shinto, and will be discussed in Chapter Two. Meiji was the symbolic architect of Japan's modernity, and it was in his name that the projects aimed at building a modern, industrialized and well-armed nation with a strong army and all the trappings of the modern state, were enacted: yet he was chosen for this role – and subsequently enshrined as a deity at a Shinto shrine – not because of any particular personal attributes but because he was the inheritor of the ancient office of Emperor, an office legitimated by Shinto myths that affirm an enduring link between the Imperial lineage and the gods of Japan, and underpinned by arcane Shinto rituals and formalities.

The nation-builders of modern Japan thus chose, as their symbol of unity, a figurehead whose position was founded in archaic myths linked to Shinto. This balancing, or integrating, of the mythic, ancient images and nature of Shinto with the modernity of an industrialized nation remains symbolic of Japan's often seemingly paradoxical blending of the traditional and the modern in one framework. Like the shrines atop modern business concerns, Meiji shrine indicates the position of Shinto as an integrative force, linked to and upholding ancient traditions, myths and customs, yet signifying the forces of modernity and development, of the assimilation and ready adoption of modern practices and technologies, and the desire for the new.

Yet, since the shrine, in its enshrinement of the spirit of an Emperor as both deity and symbol of modern Japan, also indicates the close relationship that existed between the state, the Emperor and Shinto in the earlier part of the twentieth century, it points also to the problematic issues of Shinto's position regarding the state and politics. This is an issue even more keenly indicated by the Yasukuni shrine, only a few miles away from the Meiji shrine in Tokyo, which enshrines the spirits of the war dead – including some who were executed as war criminals – and which is a focal point in a continuing dispute over the position of Shinto in the present day, and which we shall visit in Chapter Seven.

Meiji shrine is normally a quiet spot, its forested walkways providing rare respite from the hustle and bustle of the city. As such the shrine attracts not only worshippers who come to pray, often for spiritual assistance in seeking a pragmatic goal, but also passers-by who wish to find some peace and quiet. It also gets its fair share of tourists, many of whom leave their mark by offering their prayers or writing their wishes on the votive tablets known as *ema* (see Chapter Six).

At various times throughout the year, however, this normal quiet is shattered when the shrine comes alive with massive crowds of people during the various special festivals and occasions that mark the shrine's yearly ritual calendar. Like all Shinto shrines, and indeed Buddhist temples in Japan, Meiji shrine has its list of *nenjū gyōji* – yearly ritual or calendrical events – some of which are specific to the shrine in question and relate to special days or times, and others of which are widely celebrated across the country.

New Year's Festival

Such times produce the mass participatory events that are typical of the Japanese ritual calendar: throngs of people engaging in celebratory behaviour, crowding the courtyards of shrines to pray, in festive mood, to the gods. This is nowhere more readily seen than at the New Year's festival, the days at the beginning of the year when it is customary for the Japanese to make the special shrine visit known as *hatsumōde* – the first visit of the year to a shrine, to venerate and pay one's respects to the Shinto deities. During the first few days of each year, millions of Japanese (in recent years in excess of 80 million people each year, according to police statistics) perform this act, in which they thank the gods for the fortunes of the previous year, ask for help and good luck in the coming year, and acquire various talismans of good luck and of the gods' protection in the coming year.

Meiji shrine is the most heavily visited of all such places at New Year, with well over four million people passing through its *torii* in the first three days of the year, during which time this usually peaceful shrine's paths, through which the visitor can normally walk at his or her own pace, become densely packed, so that the would-be visitor can only shuffle along slowly.

These two shrines, and the *kami* that they enshrine, illustrate how Shinto is embedded in Japanese life. They also demonstrate the primary orientations of Shinto towards the world of people and their daily life: the Seidō Inari shrine, for example, with its focus on company prosperity and growth, indicates the role of the Shinto gods in providing humanly-desired needs and wishes – a wish that forms a prominent element in the prayers that people normally make during their first ritual shrine visit of the year at the New Year's festival. It is in this close relationship between the human and divine, in which the realms of the gods operate to make life fruitful for those living in this world, and in particular for the Japanese people, that the essence of Shinto is primarily located.

What Shinto Is Not!

Yet, despite its visible presence, Shinto remains puzzling and difficult to grasp. It seems to lack many of the elements that are commonly associated with other religious traditions which are useful when attempting to define what a particular religion means or stands for. As a Shinto priest once commented to me, for example, and as has been widely noted by many commentators, Shinto appears to have no set doctrines that constitute a theological basis for the tradition. Unlike, for example, Islam, Buddhism or Christianity, it has no founder or historical figure to whom its origins can be traced, no single figure of worship upon which it is focused, and no cardinal set of tenets or admonitions of behaviour akin to the Christian commandments, the Buddhist eight-fold path of right behaviour, or the five pillars of Islam, all of which outline stipulated codes of behaviour and practice expected of its members.

Nor is Shinto a 'book' religion like, for example, Sikhism, Islam or Christianity, with a specific sacred text or texts that constitute a core focus of teaching: nor, unlike Buddhism, for example, or Hinduism, does it have an organized canonical tradition of texts which serve as a set of parameters around which the religion may be framed. While there are texts that narrate myths and legends, and express ideas and ritual formats that relate to a coherent entity called 'Shinto', none has canonical authority as core texts.

Nor is Shinto a religion with universal or universalizing tendencies; native to Japan (although influenced by imported religious and cultural traditions from the mainland of Asia), its primary focuses are the people and land of Japan. In this some parallels could be drawn with other religious traditions which have a strong ethnic focus, such as Hinduism or Judaism, each of which speaks to a specific ethnic group and which emphasizes – as indeed Shinto does – a particular and special bond between a people and a religious tradition that pertains solely or primarily to that ethnic group. However, even here there are differences: while Hinduism and Judaism have developed temples and synagogues serving the numerous Hindu and Jewish communities around the world, and serve as religious focuses for Hindu and Jewish communities wherever they are, Shinto has been a rather poor traveller. Even where Shinto shrines do exist overseas, for example amongst the Japanese community in Hawaii, they hardly flourish, and may struggle to keep going.

In effect, Shinto is, and remains, a religious tradition bounded by, and closely associated with, Japan, in terms of its landscape, its history, and its myths, and in terms of the lives of the Japanese people in that physical and cultural setting.

⊙ *The Seven Gods of Good Fortune*

Chapter 1

Shinto & its Japanese Setting

Japan consists of an archipelago in which there are four main islands (Hokkaidō, Honshū, Shikoku and Kyūshū) and many thousands of smaller islands, stretching over a thousand miles in length in the Pacific Ocean. Honshū is the most populous, and contains the majority of Japan's major cities such as Tokyo, Osaka, Nagoya, and Yokohama, as well as its famed ancient capitals and cultural centres such as Nara (capital in the eighth century) and Kyoto (capital from the late eighth century until 1868).

With a population of close to 125 million people and lying on the eastern edge of the Asian mainland, with Korea and China as neighbours, Japan was the first non-Western country to industrialize. One of the few Asian countries not to have been colonized, it briefly became a colonial power in the earlier part of the twentieth century, a period in which it experienced rapid militarization as well as industrialization, and in which it sought to establish a Japanese hegemony over South-East and East Asia. In that process it invaded much of Asia, became embroiled in war with the Allies during the Second World War, and was eventually forced to surrender in August 1945, after two of its

⊗ Torii *and stone lanterns* (toro)

cities, Hiroshima and Nagasaki, had had Atomic
bombs dropped on them – the only cases so far in
history of the use of this form of warfare.

Although defeated and occupied by the Allies
for several years after 1945, Japan recovered swiftly
from the destruction of war, rebuilding its economy
and emerging as one of the economic giants of the
modern day.

Japan is known as an advanced technological
society, yet it also retains many strong underlying
traditional cultural themes as well, which have
helped provide a focus of identity, unity and

coherence in the face of the rapid changes brought about by modernization. Japan's position as culturally and physically close to mainland Asia yet separate from it, has had a profound influence on the development of Japanese culture. Just as, in the modern age, Japan has absorbed and adapted Western influences as it has developed as a modern nation, while retaining its own ethnic and traditional cultural underpinnings, so in previous ages has it both absorbed cultural influences from the continent of Asia while retaining and reinforcing its own traditions, which have thus provided both a bulwark guarding against a loss of ethnic identity, and a framework within which to incorporate and absorb external cultural influences.

❯ Absorbing External Influences

This pattern of interaction with, and of the adaptation and absorption of, external influences into Japanese culture, has been one of the recurrent features of Japanese history.

Shinto: An Indigenous Religion?

Shinto is often considered to be integral and central to that ethnic cultural tradition, and part of the indigenous cultural framework into which external influences have been assimilated. Indeed, it is often called the indigenous religion of Japan, a description that is both partially true and and partially misleading. It is true in that Shinto originated in Japan, has barely moved out of it and remains closely identified with questions of Japanese belonging and identity. This indigenous nature has been affirmed by various Japanese nationalists, scholars and Shinto priests, as well as by Shinto organizations such as *Jinja Honchō*, an affiliation of Shinto shrines which claims the support of around 75 per cent of all Shinto institutions in Japan.

Those who claim Shinto as the indigenous religious tradition of Japan are, in effect, affirming that it lies at the very heart of Japanese religiosity, providing the inspirational, spiritual core of Japan that remains at the heart of modern society and gives it its underlying stability and sense of continuity. This line of thinking, therefore, considers that there is a core of religious teachings and meanings that pre-date any cultural influences that entered Japan from the Asian mainland, and that remain basic to the Japanese spirit, unaffected by later influences from Buddhism.

This viewpoint is closely linked to nationalist sentiments which emerged in Japan particularly from the seventeenth and eighteenth centuries, as Japanese intellectuals sought to identify what was native and what was imported in their culture, and tried to assert an indigenous cultural tradition as a form of national unity in the face of external cultural pressures and influences. This intellectual tradition came to the fore in the mid-nineteenth century as Japan was forced to end the cultural isolation it had imposed on itself from the early seventeenth century onwards, and to open its doors to the outside (Western) world, a process that produced Japan's rapid modernization in the late nineteenth century under Emperor Meiji, and that led to the promotion of Shinto as a national religious tradition of unity.

Shinto: A Modern Phenomenon?

Countering those who affirm Shinto as an indigenous religion that has existed in Japan from time immemorial, are those who argue that Shinto in effect is a modern phenomenon that developed – indeed, was created – as a separate religious tradition in the nineteenth century during this period of rapid modernization. Scholars who support this view argue that, prior to this period, Shinto as a religious tradition was largely subsumed within, and subservient to, Buddhism, which has been the dominant religious force and primary shaper of the Japanese religious world ever since its entry into Japan in the sixth century CE.

This perspective holds much validity: Buddhism has become assimilated into Japan and taken on features particular to its Japanese setting, and in so doing has become a central feature of the country's religious culture, assuming responsibility for many of the most critical areas of religious activity in Japan. It has, for example, become the primary religious tradition through which deaths are handled and through which funerals and the rituals associated with death are conducted. Buddhism also brought with it promises of salvation and has

been until modern times the primary religious
vehicle through which the Japanese have sought
the possibilities of spiritual transcendence.

Until the modern period (which in effect means
until 1868 and the Meiji Restoration) Shinto shrines
and deities were often placed in a subservient
position within the courtyards of Buddhist temples,
and Buddhist priests and the figures of worship
they served frequently took precedence over Shinto
ones. Certainly, too, much of what we see today,
and that has been associated with Shinto in the
modern era, has emerged from the nineteenth
century process of the development of a separate
and identifiable tradition in which Shinto was
associated with the state and its political
structures, and in which it took on, virtually for the
first time, a position not of subservience to, but for
a period until 1945, of precedence over Buddhism.

However, both positions – asserting that
Shinto is little more than a modern invention of
tradition, or that it has existed as an independent
entity since time immemorial – are misleading.
Shinto shrines, along with various ritual practices
associated with them, existed as independent
entities prior to the nineteenth century; a
religious culture centred around native deities
with powers and attributes associated with
Japan, has existed in Japan from early times, and
much of that native culture has been incorporated
into and continued through the Shinto tradition;
and Shinto myths and legends have functioned in
religious terms for many centuries prior to the

modern period. Moreover, especially from the Middle Ages (approximately fourteenth century onwards), various Shinto theological traditions have developed in Japan to assert Shinto's independence of Buddhism.

Yet to see Shinto solely as indigenous overlooks the influence of the religious traditions that entered Japan from the sixth century CE onwards, an era in which Japan received enormous cultural infusions from the Asian mainland, including the Chinese writing system, but most notably the cultural and religious traditions of Buddhism, Confucianism and Taoism.

While only the first of these has become established in Japan as a separate and defined religious entity, both Taoism and Confucianism have also added their influences to the evolving Japanese religious tradition. Taoism in particular gave the Japanese access to practices of geomancy, divination, and forseeing the future – all of which became absorbed into the general patterns of Japanese religious activity, and are found widely in the divination and fortune-telling practices found at Shinto shrines.

Confucianism has provided a strong impetus to Japanese systems of morality, particularly in its injunctions to venerate one's ancestors and elders, and while many of its teachings on such matters have primarily been absorbed into and expressed through Buddhism in Japan, its affirmations of the importance of hierarchy and of venerating one's rulers, have been utilized in the construction of the Shinto-oriented cult of veneration of the Emperor.

Early Japanese Religion and Entry of Buddhism

It was Buddhism, however, that really developed and took root in Japan, eventually growing into a dominant Japanese religious tradition there. It was not only its teachings on morality, on ways of spiritual transcendence and enlightenment, and on the possibilities of salvation, that enhanced its appeal to the Japanese and became embedded in Japanese religious culture, but also its figures of worship, known as buddhas and bodhisattvas. These are widely believed to be able to provide worshippers with practical help and support in their lives, and it was the appeal of these figures, and the magical powers they were believed to have, that were central to Buddhism's entry to Japan.

When, in the mid-sixth century CE, the King of Paekche in Korea sought the alliance and support of the Emperor of Japan, he sent him a Buddhist statue as a present, and he accompanied it with a letter stating that this image represented a powerful new religious tradition that could provide spiritual support for the Emperor's realms and provide him with practical benefits and riches in material and spiritual terms.

At the time, Japanese religion centred around the veneration of native deities and particularly of clan deities, who were believed to be the spirits of clan ancestors, who guarded over the clan to assure its continuity and prosperity. The most prominent of such clan ancestors were those associated with the emergent Imperial dynasty, which at this time was in the process of establishing its dominance over other clan groups and thus transforming itself into the ruling power in the country.

Other native deities, especially identified with natural features such as mountains and other elements in the natural environment, were also venerated and prayed to for their protection and assistance in supporting human life. Amongst these were deities associated with such primary economic means of sustenance as agriculture and fishing. Besides being considered to be the source of good and beneficial events, such as good harvests and abundant fishing catches, the native deities were also seen as potentially dangerous, for it was believed they could cause illness and spread pestilence if offended or improperly treated.

What we would regard as natural disasters such as earthquakes and floods were regarded, in early Japanese thought, as events caused by the gods because they were angry or in response to some slight or neglect of them from the human realms. Hence one prime focus of early religious activity consisted of ritual performances and offerings de- signed to honour the gods and to make sure they would look kindly on the human world. Maintaining equilibrium and harmony with the gods so that they would in turn look after and assist human life endeavours, and not be wrathful and bring retribution, was therefore a primary element in early religious life.

Threat of New Gods and Triumph of Buddhism

The entry of the new and apparently powerful religion of Buddhism with its deities and figures of worship threatened, according to some, to challenge and upset that equilibrium, and it raised problems at the Japanese court. A major dispute arose – primarily dividing the court into two factions, ranged around prominent clans who themselves were struggling to become the prime allies of the Imperial clan – over whether the incoming gods should be worshipped, and whether so doing would offend the local gods and cause them to bring retribution on the land.

One of these two clans, the Mononobe clan, objected to the new figures of worship and championed the local gods: the other, the Soga clan, wished to venerate the new ones and argued that they and the religion, Buddhism, they represented offered a means of augmenting and developing Japan's religious and political culture.

This dispute between the two clans over the reception of Buddhism was effectively a struggle for power that was eventually won by the Soga clan after a battle for Imperial succession in 587 CE. Since both sides had invoked the deities of the religious traditions they supported, to their cause, the Soga victory appeared to show that the imported gods had triumphed over the native ones, and affirmed the Soga as the dominant clan in the land, enabling them to go forward with the promotion of Buddhism and continental culture.

The Soga Prince Shōtoku (573–621), son of Emperor Yōmei, is regarded as the 'father of Buddhism' in Japan, and in his period of influence he built many important Buddhist temples and promoted Buddhism as the primary religion of the Japanese state – a position it held for much of the following 1,200 years.

However, the apparent victory of the new, imported religion did not overwhelm and sweep aside the native one, which proved remarkably resilient and capable of adaptation to the new circumstances. Shōtoku recognized this when he paid homage to the native tradition and affirmed, in a proclamation in 607, the importance of venerating the native gods of Japan.

Development and Meaning of Word 'Shinto'

The concept of Shinto itself, in many respects, came about as a result of the entry of Buddhism into Japan, for the loosely structured native religious tradition had no specific name, nor any coordinated elements, until well after the arrival of Buddhism, when it became necessary to identify the local tradition in the context of the foreign, so as to define what was local, thereby giving both a name and form to the native tradition.

The term 'Shinto', therefore, was developed in order to identify the native tradition centred on the local deities, or *kami,* and it stands in contrast to *Bukkyō,* the Japanese word for Buddhism. *Bukkyō* means 'the teaching of the Buddha', and like other religious traditions whose names have been translated into Japanese, there is an emphasis here on the concept of 'teachings' (*kyō*).

SHIN
KAMI

TŌ
MICHI

By contrast, the term 'Shinto' indicates not a 'teaching' (i.e. a religion with a formulated doctrinal system) but a 'way' or course of action. The two Chinese ideograms that make up the term Shinto can, like most Sino-Japanese ideograms, be read in more than one way in Japanese, depending on the context. The ideogram *shin* means a deity, and may also be read as *kami* (the standard term for a Shinto deity), while the second ideogram can also be read as *michi*, and means a way or path. Thus the word Shinto means the 'way of the gods', with the primary emphasis being on the first of the two ideograms, for Shinto is a religious tradition that is intimately associated with, and centred on, the gods, or *kami*.

The term Shinto was first used in an eighth century text, the *Nihon Shoki* (known also as the *Nihongi*, 'the chronicles of Japan'), a semi-mythical history of Japan and its Emperors produced in 720 CE. This text and a further text, the *Kojiki* ('Records of Ancient Matters'), produced in 712 CE, were closely associated with the production of a sense of Japanese identity and cultural independence, and narrated myths and mythical histories relating to the origins of Japan and to the activities of the *kami* in such respects.

Chapter 2

Kami, Myths
& Meanings

The Japanese ideogram which is read as *shin*
in the term Shinto, is more commonly known in its
alternative reading of *kami*. The term itself is often
translated as 'god' or 'deity', but in English
language commentaries, is often left in the
Japanese, since terms like god and deity do not
wholly convey the meanings associated with *kami*.
Japanese does not differentiate between singulars
and plurals, so the term *kami* may refer to either a
specific *kami*, or to pluralities. In general terms,
however, the term and concept of *kami* is a plural
one, for there are enormous, potentially infinite,
numbers of *kami* associated with Japan and the
Shinto tradition.

A popular phrase speaks of Japan as the country
of *yao yorozu no kami*, a term which literally means
8 million *kami*, but in reality implies infinite
numbers, for all and any manifestation of nature,
natural object or expression of life may be
considered to express or manifest the nature of
kami. In such terms, *kami* indicates or refers to a
natural force or manifestation of energy or life-force
within given objects or places, and to spirits and
signs of spiritual energy within the world. It can

The meotoiwa *('wedded rocks') at Futamigaura near Ise, with straw* torii, *which symbolize the union of Izanagi and Izanami*

also refer to, and includes, the divinities which, according to Shinto myths, gave life to the earth and which also produce fields of spiritual energy that can influence aspects of human life, as well as to the spirits of humans who have been influential or gifted in life and whose spirits may be transformed into *kami* afterwards so that their gifts may continue to benefit the world.

This breadth of meanings indicates a very animistic culture, in which all manner of phenomena may be attributed with spiritual force: as a famous definition by the eighteenth-century Japanese thinker and scholar Motoori

⌄ Yasaka shrine, Kyoto

Norinaga states, it is not only the divinities of Japanese sacred texts and myths that are considered as *kami*, for anything – humans, animals, trees, plants, rocks, mountains, seas – which appears impressive, inspires a sense of awe or exhibits a life-force, may be *kami*. In other words, anything in the phenomenal world may be a *kami*, and manifest the nature and spirit of, or be the abode of, a *kami*.

Forms of *Kami*

Within this broad spectrum, one can make some further definitions and differentiations between types of *kami*. For example, one can identify important *kami* associated with the legends of creation and the construction of Japan as set out in Shinto myths (see below), such as Amaterasu, the Sun Goddess. Other figures from Japanese mythology, including the spirits of many of the earliest named Emperors in the *Nihon Shoki* (who were figures more of myth than historical reality), are also venerated as *kami*, such as the spirit of the mythical third-century CE Emperor Ojin. Ojin was a great hero in Japanese myths, and as a valiant warrior his spirit is venerated as Hachiman, a *kami* of war and victory, at thousands of shrines throughout Japan.

There are also regional and clan deities, many of which originated as guardian deities of the various kinship groups or clans around which early Japanese society was organized. Such clan gods (known as *ujigami*) often were the spirits of clan ancestors, but could also be local community deities who guarded over the people who were born or who lived within the local area or region over which the deity presided.

Other important deities included the spirits of humans who, due to their position and influence in life, were believed to continue to have an influence afterwards, and who became venerated as gods. This type of deity (*hitogami*, or gods who derive from humans) remained highly important in Shinto, and many of the principal Shinto deities, such as Tenjin, the god of education, are of this sort: humans whose qualities in life made them a suitable focus for veneration afterwards.

Tenjin was, in life, a great scholar named Sugawara no Michizane, who lived in the ninth century. He was exiled because of court intrigues, and died unhappily in exile in 903 CE. Shortly after his death, a series of plagues and other natural disasters struck the then capital of Kyoto. People at the time saw these disasters as being caused by his unhappy and vengeful spirit, and in order to placate it, Michizane was posthumously honoured and his spirit enshrined and venerated as the *kami* Tenjin (literally '*kami* of Heaven') at Dazaifu in Kyūshū (where he had been exiled) and in Kyoto. Because of his learning in life, he is especially venerated as a *kami* of education, and there are now shrines throughout the country dedicated to his spirit.

While certain *kami* are clearly more widely

venerated and have more shrines dedicated to them than others, Shinto nonetheless does not posit a fixed hierarchy of *kami*, nor does it have one founder deity who is at the heart of its concepts of creation. Shinto, unlike many other religious traditions which have creation myths, has no founder deity or set hierarchy: although Amaterasu, the Sun Goddess and legendary ancestor of the Imperial clan, emerges as the most important deity, she is not the initial creator of the world, and other *kami* also continue to have their own powers and areas of influence.

One should note that not all *kami* are native, for some important deities venerated in the Shinto tradition have come from outside Japan. Buddhism, in particular, assimilated a number of Hindu deities into its pantheon during its early period in India, and many of these have been transplanted along with Buddhism to Japan.

One of the most popular of these deities is Benten (also known as Benzaiten), a deity highly popular among artists and musicians, as a patroness and guardian deity of the arts, whose roots can be traced back to the Hindu deity Saraswati, who was absorbed into Buddhism as it began its spread eastward across Asia. Benten is interesting also because she is a good example of the close interactions between Shinto and Buddhism, for she may be found venerated at both Shinto shrines and Buddhist temples.

Inari, the rice deity and modern business god, is another deity that falls into a similar category of being venerated in both Shinto and Buddhist contexts. Besides these types of deity, there are many *kami* with highly localized powers or presences, that may, according to Shinto belief, have potential influence within their localized spheres.

Relationship of Humans and *Kami*

What the general notion of *kami* demonstrates is a highly pluralistic and animistic world view, in which the phenomenal world is seen as permeated by and given life by a spiritual world, in which various manifestations of life forces (*kami*) are present. This world view is reiterated also in Shinto myths, which depict the world as having been brought alive by the acts of the *kami*, and it indicates a world in which humans and *kami* are extremely close.

Indeed, Shinto's world view suggests that humans who contribute to the enrichment of life may become *kami*, as was the case with Michizane, or with clan founders or ancestors who became *ujigami*, and thereby continue to assist in the life of this world. Moreover, in this human–*kami* relationship, it is humans who play the crucial role of recognizing the presence of the *kami* in a natural feature, or as a result of some event or manifestation. It is also human beings who are operative in transforming spirits into *kami* through the process of recognition, veneration and enshrinement, as was seen by the transformation of the angry spirit of Michizane into Tenjin.

The closeness of humans and *kami* is also emphasized in the various legends and myths associated with the *kami* that are outlined below, and which paint a picture of *kami* as manifesting an often extremely human nature. Like the gods of Greek myths, the Japanese *kami* may copulate and procreate, argue, fight, have ambitions, seek to be the most important deity, and occasionally sulk when they do not get their way. They are earthy, and manifest a bawdy humour, enjoy life, get drunk and generally behave in a very human way. They may also exhibit a potential for malevolence and the capacity to be dangerous and harmful to life: indeed, it was for these reasons of potential danger that Michizane was transformed into and venerated as the *kami* Tenjin.

Other potentially dangerous and disruptive deities include Susanoo, the brother of Amaterasu the Sun Goddess, who, in the legends outlined below, behaves extremely badly and exhibits a potential for destruction. Susanoo is venerated at numerous shrines in Japan, prominent amongst them being the Yasaka shrine in Kyoto (whose major festival, one of the great festivals of Japan, the Gion *matsuri* festival, is dedicated to Susanoo) as a protector against misfortunes and disasters: a striking case of how veneration and homage directed towards a deity are believed to be able to transform or appease that deity into manifesting its potentially benevolent sides. Like humans, *kami* need to be treated correctly and they demand appropriate veneration, a point that

» Some Important *Kami* in Shinto Tradition

Amaterasu – Sun Goddess, born after Izanagi's ritual purification according to myth, and associated according to myth also with the Japanese Emperor; venerated in particular at the Inner shrine at Ise.

Benten – *kami* of music and the arts: also worshipped in Buddhist forms, Benten's origins can be traced to the Indian goddess Saraswati. Associated with water, her shrines are often on islands – such as the Enoshima Benten shrine south of Kamakura, which stands on a tiny island joined to the shoreline by a short bridge, or the island of Chikubushima in Lake Biwa, which has both a Buddhist temple and a Shinto shrine, both dedicated to Benten.

Ebisu – a popular *kami* of prosperity associated in modern times with shopkeepers and small businesses; often depicted as a smiling, bearded fisherman, he is especially popular in the Osaka region, where two of his most important shrines, Nishinomiya Ebisu shrine and Imamiya Ebisu shrine, are located.

Hachiman – spirit of the legendary Emperor Ojin, this was once an imperial clan *kami*. Originally a god of war, Hachiman is popular today because of its associations with victory, and hence with success.

is highly central to Shinto religious practices, and especially festivals and rituals, which centre on humouring and honouring the *kami*, themes we shall look at in Chapter Six.

Shinto, as this outline of its figures of worship suggests, is very much a this-worldly focused religious tradition, centred on the relationship of *kami* and humans. It is true that in early Japanese

Inari – deity originally of rice but in modern times also a *kami* of business and production; it is also worshipped in a Buddhist form and in Buddhist temples as well. Its main shrines include Fushimi Inari in Kyoto and Yutoku Inari in Kyushu.

Izanami and **Izanagi** – female and male *kami* central to Shinto myths of creation of Japan.

Konpira – *kami* associated with the sea, both in terms of safety and economic activities. Thus Konpira is a patron of sailors (and by extension, other travellers, including space travellers: see Chapter Six), fishermen and of ships and shipbuilders.

Susanoo – Amaterasu's brother, the *kami* of the wind: a dangerous *kami* capable of inflicting disasters, but if properly venerated, able to protect against such problems. Amongst its main shrines is the Yasaka shrine in Kyoto.

Tenjin – *kami* of education: the enshrined spirit of Sugawara no Michizane, a ninth-century Japanese noted for learning. Tenjin shrines are found throughout the country and are especially popular with students.

cosmology there were notions of other realms existing besides this. Early Japanese thought conceived of three other worlds: *Takamagahara* (which translates as the plain of high heaven); *Yomi no kuni* (the underworld); and *Tokoyo no kuni* (the other world: literally, the world across the water). The first, Takamagahara, was the abode of the *kami* and was seen as similar to though better than the human world; the second was dark and polluted, the realms where the spirits of the dead dwelt; and the third was vaguely conceived of as a realm of abundant and eternal life.

None of these realms, however, ever assumed the status of a higher, transcendent realm in comparison with the human world, and, indeed, they later ceased to be considered as important, to the extent that modern Shinto barely if ever speaks of them. Partially this was because Buddhism's own conceptions of other worlds relating to the spirits of the dead and to possible paradises, supplanted the existing native concepts, but more particularly because Shinto, as a tradition centred around the relationship of *kami* and humans, was always primarily a religion of this world, and in particular a religion associated with the land and people of Japan and their relations to, and links with, the *kami*.

All the themes mentioned above, and many more relating to crucial concepts in Shinto, are manifested in the corpus of legends and myths associated with the *kami*; in order to illustrate further some of the essential meanings of Shinto as they pertain to the *kami*, we will now turn to Shinto myths and their meanings.

Shinto Foundation Myths

The Japanese term *shinwa*, which is usually translated as myth or myths, literally means 'tales/stories about the *kami*', and, indeed, Shinto myths are most certainly stories that depict the deeds and activities of the *kami*, and that, in so doing, impart messages about the nature of the religious tradition they belong to and the world they are associated with.

Myths have played a major part in the development and teachings of Shinto, not only in outlining the roles, nature and powers of the *kami*, but in highlighting Shinto's primary orientation as a religious tradition associated with this world, and in establishing some of the basic teachings and perspectives upon which Shinto is founded. Some of these myths and the messages they impart have also been extremely important in the promotion of Japanese nationalist sentiments, for in early Shinto myths there is much emphasis on a special relationship between the *kami* and the Japanese people, land, and the Imperial household. The notions that are expressed in such myths have been especially central to the nineteenth- and twentieth-century perceptions and uses of Shinto as a religion associated with Japanese nationalism.

Shinto myths exist at a number of levels, from overarching myths that provide legendary explanations of creation and of the origins of the Japanese people, to localized stories outlining the stories of particular shrines and the powers of specific *kami* enshrined at them. It is especially with these myths relating to creation that we are able to see the formation of the broader parameters of Shinto.

Perhaps the most famous Shinto myths of all are narrated in the texts that were produced in the early eighth century, after almost two centuries of influence from Chinese culture and of Buddhist influence. In other words, the texts and the native tradition about which they speak had themselves been influenced by the imported religious and cultural traditions of the continent: as we saw earlier, Taoism and Confucianism also had an impact on the formation and development of the native tradition, just as did Buddhism.

It was at this period that the Japanese Imperial household had truly established its authority as ruler of a Japanese state centred around the Imperial court and its administrative structures. In order to augment its authority, to provide itself with a historical background that underpinned its right to rule, and also to create a sense of identity for the newly emergent nation and culture – one that affirmed its ethnic origins rather than its cultural traditions imbibed from abroad – the Imperial household oversaw the production of the two texts mentioned in the previous chapter, the *Kojiki* ('records of ancient times') in 712 CE and the *Nihon Shoki* or *Nihongi* ('the chronicles of Japan') in 720 CE.

These texts purported to narrate Japan's origins and early history and, in the *Nihongi*, the chronicles of the Imperial household and of past Emperors. Though largely mythical in nature, recounting myths that depicted the country as a sacred land created by the *kami*, and the Imperial family as descendants of these *kami* (a descent that legitimated their right to rule), many of the themes treated in these texts, especially in the *Kojiki's* myths of creation, express some basic themes and meanings central to Shinto through the ages, and which operate as a form of doctrinal structure for the religion.

The myths of the *Kojiki* relate to the creation not of the universe but the land of Japan and ultimately its rulers and people: as such they provide a creation myth specific, just as is Shinto itself, to the Japanese land and people. In such terms, for Shinto the universal is centred on Japan and the Japanese.

Story of Izanagi and Izanami

According to the *Kojiki*, as the universe began, a number of deities came into existence, and they in turn produced two further deities, Izanagi (male) and Izanami (female), who were given the task of producing the land of Japan from the primordial swamps. Standing on the bridge of heaven, they dipped a sacred sword into the sea, stirred it and from this came forth the island of Onogoro, the original land of Japan. The two deities then set about peopling this island with deities that would live in and give life to the land.

The process of giving birth to these *kami* reflects a remarkably human dimension, and a preoccupation with copulation, blood and distress, which culminates in the death of Izanami as she is giving birth to the *kami* of fire. This death, besides emphasizing the inherent dangers of elements such as fire, shows that *kami* also may be finite and subject to death.

Death, especially premature death, as it is

depicted here and as it is viewed in Shinto, is a disruptive event that unsettles the natural order and can lead to chaos and strife. This is emphasized when Izanagi, displaying how *kami* have emotions akin to those of humans, grieves over his wife's death and, wishing not to be separated from her, follows her to the underworld.

However, when he reaches the underworld he encounters a horrific scene which emphasizes just how terrible death and decay are in the Shinto perspective, for he comes across Izanami's rotting and maggot-infested body, full of the decay of death. Izanami attempts to drag her erstwhile husband to her realms, which are now the realms of death. In this action she manifests the nature of the recently departed spirits of the dead as perceived in early Japanese religious thought, as lonely, and therefore desirous of the company of their fellows and especially their close kin. The spirits of the recent dead are thus highly dangerous, and, because of their loneliness and sense of abandonment by the living, also potentially malevolent.

Izanagi, faced with this apparition, flees back to the land of the living, but is pursued by his wife. To prevent her from entering again the world of the living, he rolls a rock across the entry to the underworld, thereby drawing a line between the worlds of the living and dead. This formal and symbolic ritual separation of the worlds of the living and dead is, however, challenged by Izanami, who manifests the resentments of the spirits of the dead against the living by demanding that the rock be removed and the dead be given access to the land of the living. When Izanagi refuses, Izanami threatens to bring death and destruction to the world by taking 1,000 lives every day: her husband responds by saying if she does, he will create 1,500 souls a day. In this pledge, he clearly asserts the primacy of life over death, and commits the *kami* henceforth to the support, maintenance and promulgation of life in this world.

Heavenly Siblings: Story of Amaterasu and Susanoo

After this terrifying encounter, Izanagi bathes to purify himself of the pollutions of death, and through this ritual purification he alone gives birth to a number of new *kami*. The ritual, therefore, has regenerative effects as well, emphasizing the lifegiving powers of the *kami*. Amongst the deities thus born are Amaterasu, the Sun Goddess, and her brother, Susanoo, the *kami* of the wind. Izanagi then gives Amaterasu ascendancy over the land: Susanoo, believing he should have this vital role, becomes angry and insults his sister, with the result that his father banishes him.

However, as we saw earlier, Susanoo remains an important and powerful *kami*, fearful because of his potential wrath, but known and venerated for his powers of protection against disasters. After this Izanagi largely retires from the picture, his part in the evolving myths of development, complete.

When Amaterasu is insulted by Susanoo in his rage, she in turn sulks and withdraws from the world, hiding in a cave. The disappearance of the sun causes the world to go dark and gloomy, distressing the other *kami* and causing them to plead, unsuccessfully, with Amaterasu to come back and restore light to the world. At first the *kami* are

unable to persuade her to return until a female deity performs a bawdy and sexual dance before the cave; the other *kami* laugh uproariously at this, which causes Amaterasu to look out to see what is going on: she is immediately seized and dragged forth by the gods, so that light is restored and she returns to her rightful and central place in the world.

⊙ *Amaterasu, the Sun Goddess, emerging from her cave.*
From a Japanese painting in the British Museum

Here, too, we see examples of the human attributes of the *kami*, from Amaterasu's sulking, which causes her withdrawal, and her inquisitiveness, which brings her back to the world, to the *kami's* enjoyment of bawdy entertainment. The importance of entertaining the *kami* subsequently has become a central feature of Shinto ritual processes, with the dance of the female *kami* being re-enacted, in a solemn and dignified form, by shrine maidens known as *miko* during Shinto rites and festivals (see Chapter Five).

Myths of Imperial Descent

Subsequently, the world is pacified, and order restored, with Amaterasu's importance as the provider of light recognized. This does not mean she is all-powerful, as indeed, her seizure and enforced return to the world, show: she must take note of the other *kami*, who can assert authority over her if need be, and must serve the world through her role as the Sun Goddess. Amaterasu also produces her own offspring; her grandson, Ninigi, is then given the mandate to rule earth (i.e. Japan) and in so doing, is entrusted with a set of sacred objects, a mirror (the symbol of Amaterasu), sword and jewel. These in turn are passed down to Ninigi's greatgrandson Jimmu, who in these mythical histories is designated as the first Emperor of Japan: it is the Emperor's task and duty to guard the three items, mirror, sword and jewel, which together constitute the sacred imperial regalia of Japan.

The story told above is a very truncated outline of some of the complex myths narrated in these early texts, but this outline highlights some important structural ideas for Shinto, especially the relationship between the *kami* and the people and land of Japan. In the myths the Imperial household is depicted as descending from Amaterasu, and it is this divine descent that, in traditional and nationalist eyes, confers legitimacy on the Imperial household, and that has been used, at certain times in Japanese history, to argue that Emperors, as descendants of the *kami*, possess a divine nature. This was the position adopted by the state and Shinto in the first half of the twentieth century, and only renounced after Japan's defeat in war.

Jimmu is counted, in Imperial lineages, as the first Emperor, assuming the mantle of Emperor in 660 BCE, a date that has no historical substance, for Jimmu remains just a figure of myth. The sacred regalia he was entrusted with are, according to Shinto belief, enshrined in three places: the mirror at the Ise shrine, the sword at Atsuta shrine in Nagoya, and the jewel at the Imperial palace. The myths, as we have seen, depict the land as being created and given life by the *kami*, thus affirming a special relationship of land and deities: in effect, the land is alive with, and the special preserve of, the *kami*, while in the myths the Japanese people descend from the *kami* produced by Izanagi and Izanami.

Basic Themes of Shinto

The *Kojiki* myths thus sacralize Japan and its
people, as descendants of the *kami*. The role and
duties of the *kami* are also expressed forcibly
through the myths: to give life to the land, to
maintain that life and to focus on the happiness
of people in this world. The myths emphasize
the importance of spiritual and ritual purification,
as in Izanagi's bathing after his encounter in
the underworld, through which process evils
are eradicated and new life is produced.
Shinto's abhorrence of, and where possible
avoidance of, the impurities of death are also
seen in these interactions.

While the above myths are extremely important in
terms of the structures and meanings of Shinto, they
are but part of a wider corpus which reflects the
virtually infinite numbers of *kami* and the vast
numbers of shrines found in Japan. Each shrine also
has its own founding myths or legends which narrate
how its particular *kami* became associated with, or
manifested itself at, that place, and which proclaim
what particular powers that *kami* has in that place. In
such terms, myths function not only at national and
overarching levels, as with the myths narrated in the
Kojiki, to provide meaning and frameworks for Shinto
at the highest levels, but operate, too, at more local
ones to endow a particular location with a sacred
presence and to inscribe it with a sacred power that
can be tapped or called upon by those who visit the

place, and those whose community the shrine's *kami* serves and protects, to assist and support them in the fruitful pursuance of their lives.

❯❯ Maintaining Life in This World

From these myths pictures emerge of Shinto as a religious tradition focused specifically around the Japanese land and its people, and their relationship with a set of life giving and life-maintaining spiritual entities – the *kami.* It is thus concerned especially with the maintenance of life in this world, with the maintenance of correct relations between the *kami* and people, and with the upholding and furtherance of life in this world.

Perceiving a life-force (in the form of *kami*) present in the phenomena of the natural world, Shinto expresses a reverence for nature – although it has to be emphasized that this reverence for the world of nature has not translated into a coherently expressed Shinto stance against the economic exploitation of nature, or prevented the development of environmentally-damaging economic activities in Japan.

Shinto also expresses a concern with the avoidance of the taboos and pollutions caused by untoward events such as death, and a horror at, and fear of, dislocations in the natural order of things. In order to right the imbalances caused by such unsettling and polluting incidents, we see an emphasis, which is crucial to Shinto practice, on ritual action, which serves as a means of eradicating impurities and restoring balance to the world. Purification rituals are especially emphasized in this respect, and in Shinto, rituals thus serve as a moral force through which the correct nature and balance of relationships essential to the smooth running of the world are expressed.

In such rituals, too, the relationships of humans and *kami* are expressed, and while we have seen that the role of the *kami* is to uphold and enhance life in this world, they also require and merit correct treatment. As the myths show, they can be fickle and have distinctly human traits: hence they like, and need, to be feted.

❯ Religious Practice and Purification

A crucial aspect of Shinto religious practice involves the correct performance of rituals that honour the gods, and need to be carried out by people in a ritually pure state (which is why water fountains are found at the entrance to shrines, to enable worshippers to ritually purify themselves prior to praying) and usually accompanied by offerings made to the *kami*.

These, then, are some of the basic themes and principles of Shinto, expressed in myths and focused around the relationship between the *kami* and the human world – a relationship that is brought to life through rituals and other such practices, especially within the ambit of Shinto shrines. These are issues that will be examined in subsequent chapters, where we look at the rituals and at practices relating to, and associated with, the *kami* and their places of worship. Before we come to such descriptions of contemporary Shinto shrine life, however, we should first turn again to the relationship between Shinto and Buddhism, and to further examinations of the historical development of Shinto.

Chapter 3

Shinto in Japanese Religious History

Shinto Buddhist Interactions

Shinto's development in Japan, and the roles it performs, cannot be fully understood outside of its interactions with Buddhism. From the outset these two traditions have been locked together in a close relationship in which there has been much mutual interaction and influence, and we have already seen how the entry of Buddhism into Japan played a part in the development of a recognizable Shinto tradition.

At times, the interactions have been antagonistic, as supporters and priests of the two traditions have sought to assert their own tradition over the other. Over the centuries, Buddhist and Shinto adherents engaged in arguments, each claiming their figures of worship were the more important. The Buddhists were successful in asserting the universality of their religion, and in thus portraying Shinto and its *kami* merely as a local tradition, and in establishing Buddhism as the primary religion of the Japanese state.

❯❯ Todaiji Temple

If was state patronage which built the great Buddhist temple of Todaiji and its central image, the great Buddha, which formed the focal point of the new capital, Nara, when it was built in the eighth century. At the same time, the state built a series of Buddhist temples known as *kokubunji* throughout the country, with one in each province, as official state temples affiliated to Todaiji and representing a national network of state-sponsored Buddhism.

⊙ *Shinto priests purifying an offering from the Emperor*
at the Great Shrine of Ise

Yet, even at this period, when Buddhism appeared to triumph and become the state religion, Shinto showed its continuing importance, in its role as legitimator of the Imperial household's ascendancy and as supporter of national myths. In practical terms, too, the association between the Shinto *kami* and the land so clearly expressed in the *Kojiki* myths, manifested itself in practical terms in relation to the building of Buddhist temples. When the great Buddha Hall at Todaiji was being built, Shinto priests proclaimed that the *kami* Hachiman had spoken in an oracle, expressing his fears for the safety of the great Buddha, and his desire to have his shrine moved into the Todaiji precincts so that he could protect the statue. It was a cunning move by the Shinto adherents to 'discover' this oracle, for the wishes of Hachiman, as a *kami* who was the spirit of a (legendary) former Emperor, were hardly likely to be ignored by the Emperor.

Hachiman thus became adopted as the guardian deity of the temple, and Hachiman protective shrines were also built throughout the land to protect the *kokubunji* temples. The role of the *kami* as native deities concerned with the land of Japan, and as protectors and guardians of all that stands on the land, was thus extended to Buddhist temples as well.

In the present day, too, the Shinto *kami* and their priests continue to command this function of being the guardians of the land and all that is built upon it. New building projects in Japan usually involve a Shinto ritual known as a *jichinsai*, or ground-breaking ceremony, in which the local *kami* are placated and their cooperation is sought for the successful completion and safe continuity of the structure.

The principle established through Hachiman's assumption of guardianship and protection of the great Buddha thus bound the two traditions together, and while Buddhism might claim it was superior to the *kami*, it still needed their protection, a pattern that has continued to the present day. It is a common sight in Buddhist temple courtyards, for example, to come across a *torii* and shrine, in

⊙ *Kasuga shrine, Nara*

which the temple's guardian *kami* resides, and to
note a Shinto presence at Buddhist locations.
Indeed, if one enters the courtyard of Todaiji in
Nara one can see clear and continuing evidence of
this Shinto presence for there is a *torii* and shrine
dedicated to Benten situated on the right as one
approaches the Buddha Hall.

This emergent close relationship between the
two also saw the development of shrine–temple
complexes, such as that at Nara involving the great
Buddhist temple Kōfukuji and the nearby Kasuga
shrine, both under the patronage of the powerful
Fujiwara clan. Kasuga shrine was originally the
Fujiwara's clan shrine but through their power and
prestige became one of the region's most important
shrines, and the status of its *kami* was enhanced
through its links to the powerful Kōfukuji temple.

Such shrine–temple complexes, as well as
the development of close bonds between specific
temples and shrines, became a common theme from
this era onwards, as did the notion that the *kami*
and buddhas in effect were two sides of a similar
coin. This interaction was primarily developed by
the Buddhists who argued that their figures of
worship were universal, and the *kami* merely local
(and therefore inferior) manifestations of them, but
it produced mutually beneficial results: local people
often more readily accepted the newer (Buddhist)
figures of worship because they appeared to be
sanctioned by the local *kami* who served as their
protectors, while often, in turn, the *kami*'s powers
were enhanced by association with Buddhism.

Inari is a good example of this concept. It was originally a local *kami* in Fushimi in south Kyoto. When the important Buddhist temple Tōji was established in the vicinity, in the early ninth century, with Imperial patronage, by Kūkai, the founder of the Shingon sect of Buddhism and one of the great and famous Buddhist priests of Japan, he adopted the local *kami* Inari as the temple's protector. The Shingon sect founded by Kūkai became one of the dominant religious forces of the land, and Inari's status increased accordingly, while its adoption by Shingon enabled it to acquire increased spiritual powers, until it became one of the most prominent and powerful *kami* of the country. The original shrine associated with it, at Fushimi, has become one of the most important shrines in Japan.

Inari's close association with the powerful esoteric Shingon Buddhist sect not only increased Inari's powers but gave it a Buddhist guise in addition to its Shinto one. Indeed, two of the most important Inari centres of worship in Japan are at Buddhist temples – Toyokawa Inari in Aichi prefecture, and Saijō Inari near the city of Okayama in western Japan – where Inari is venerated in a Buddhist form. As such, Inari is a good example both of the enhanced powers that *kami* could achieve through association with Buddhism and of how Shinto's relationship with Buddhism can enrich its tradition and enhance the powers of its *kami*, and of how the two traditions have interacted in Japan.

Watarai Shinto

Gradually, Shinto resistance grew to this process of virtual amalgamation and interaction, particularly from the Kamakura (1185–1333) period onwards, since the effect was to place Shinto in a subservient position to Buddhism. Predominant among those seeking to reverse the tide of Buddhist dominance were the priests of the Outer Shrine (Gekū) at Ise, the location of perhaps the most important shrines in all Japan, centred on Amaterasu.

The hereditary priests at the Gekū were members of the Watarai family, and they actively sought to develop a doctrinally focused form of Shinto centred on Ise and accessible not just to the Imperial family (who were the main shrine patrons) but the masses. They developed what became known as Watarai Shinto, a system that stressed the virtues of purity and honesty, and emphasized rites of purification.

Watarai Shinto asserted that for the Japanese, the *kami* at Ise were paramount and it was through them that one could attain spiritual purification and advancement. To accomplish such purification they advocated the pilgrimage to Ise (*Ise mairi*: the term *mairi* means to visit a shrine or temple, and is widely used to indicate a pilgrimage) as a vital religious practice for all. Pilgrimages to Ise became a major religious practice, especially from around the seventeenth century, and were often occasions of mass participation.

In normal years in the Tokugawa period, it is

estimated that as many as half a million people would make the pilgrimage to Ise, bringing back with them to their home villages the sacred amulets and talismans of the shrines to serve as symbols of good luck and as objects of veneration in their villages. Ise was also the focus of even greater mass pilgrimages known as *okage mairi* at periodic intervals during the Tokugawa period, in which several million people participated: probably the greatest of these were in 1771 and 1830.

However, although various lineages of priests sought to promote Shinto as a religious system the equal of Buddhism, developed ritual practices accessible to the wider populace, and stimulated popular mass devotion to the *kami*, Shinto was unable to match Buddhism in terms of coordinated and coherent doctrinal structures. Buddhism continued to be the dominant force in the Japanese religious world, a position emphasized during the Tokugawa period (1600–1868) when it became the de facto state religion and all Japanese were obliged by law to swear allegiance to and be members of a local Buddhist temple.

Meiji Restoration and Shinto

Shinto shrines were generally subservient to temples in this period, a picture that changed dramatically after the Meiji Restoration of 1868, when the new government, seeking to strengthen a sense of Japanese identity at a period of rapid change, turned against Buddhism, partially because of its close links with the former regime, and adopted Shinto as a religion of state. In this process, the myths linking Japan, the *kami* and the Imperial family were emphasized, veneration of the the Emperor (who was claimed to be a *kami*) promoted and later enforced, and important Shinto shrines given state patronage.

The government enforced a policy known as *shinbutsu bunri*, separating the *kami* and buddhas, in which shrines were divested of Buddhist influences, forcibly if need be, and placed in an ascendant role. In the process thousands of Buddhist temples and images were destroyed, and many other Buddhist figures were assimilated to, and incorporated into, Shinto shrines.

Although Shinto thus assumed a position of power, this state support did not always work to its benefit, at least at local levels. Small, local shrines in particular, were amalgamated or forced to become subservient to major ones promoting the Imperial cult, and the community aspects of Shinto, as they related to local *kami* and their local community of followers, were subjugated to the nationalist aims and centralizing wishes of the state religion.

State sponsorship and use of Shinto in the latter nineteenth and earlier part of the twentieth century has in retrospect been termed 'state Shinto' (*kokka Shintō*), and the term is often understood to incorporate the state-centred promotion of Shinto rituals and of a national ideology and unity centred on total allegiance to the Emperor who, venerated as a *kami*, was the dominant symbol of Japanese nationalism. The government also crushed any religious opposition to this ideology, which became part of its expansionist military policies in the lands it seized, colonized, and brought war and destruction to, especially in the period 1931–45.

Post-War Era and Shinto Disestablishment

It was because of the uses of Shinto by the state, and because of the state patronage of Shinto as a virtual arm of the state, that when Japan was defeated and occupied in 1945, its system of government was thoroughly revised, and new policies concerning religion were inaugurated. Shinto was disestablished: in other words, its state patronage was removed and it became free of both state support and state control. Moreover, in the constitution of 1946 Japanese citizens were, for the first time, constitutionally guaranteed freedom of religion, all state sponsorship of religion was abolished and Japan became a fully secular state, with all bonds between the state and religion dissolved.

In 1946, also, the then-Emperor made a broadcast renouncing the notion that he was a *kami*: henceforth the Emperor was to be a constitutional figure, a human embodiment and symbol of state, not a divine being in whose name people could be forced to act. Such changes have not been universally accepted, and many nationalists and supporters of Shinto have campaigned to restore the former links between Shinto and the state and, especially, to maintain state funding of some Shinto shrines. These are some of the most controversial issues in post-war Japan and will be discussed later in Chapter Seven.

These post-war constitutional changes have caused Shinto some problems, particularly in the loss of financial support. Moreover, especially in the immediate aftermath of the war, Shinto, due to its close associations with the state that had led Japan to defeat, had become severely discredited. In subsequent years the shrines have sought to rectify the position in many ways. One has been to develop a new organization of Shinto shrines, known as Jinja Honchō (The Association of Shinto Shrines), which has become the main coordinating organization for Shinto in Japan.

Regarding the shrines of Ise as the apex of Shinto, Jinja Honchō promotes Shinto as a national system of faith in the *kami* and emphasizes the importance of Shinto rituals and festivals as occasions for bringing people and *kami* together in mutual respect, and emphasizes Shinto's veneration of nature.

Besides the development of Jinja Honchō, individual shrines have sought to emphasize the ritual and festive aspects of Shinto both on community and individual levels, promoting such events as festivals, as well as individual acts of worship, such as pilgrimages, and have asserted the role of the *kami* in providing blessings at critical moments in the life-cycle of individuals and communities. All these themes will be looked at in subsequent chapters, but first we will briefly look at the general patterns of Shinto–Buddhist interaction as it has evolved in Japan.

Dynamics of Japanese Religious World

Although the two traditions of Shinto and Buddhism have a history of conflicts and disputes over the preeminence of one over the other, and can be distinguished from each other in many respects, they also share many areas of mutual accommodation, and it is such features that are amongst the most striking elements in the world of Japanese religion. At popular levels of practice, indeed, it is often hard to see where their dividing lines really lie.

In general terms, when praying for the benefits and graces believed to be dispensed by figures of worship from these two traditions, Japanese petitioners often barely differentiate between *kami* and buddhas, and they may petition or pray before each in a remarkably similar fashion. Indeed, the Japanese often use a single term *shinbutsu* (made up of the ideograms for *kami* and *butsu*, buddha) to signify both forms of benefit-granting figures of worship. Furthermore, they are likely to pray both at Shinto shrines and Buddhist temples, and to participate in the ritual activities of both, without considering there to be any conflict in seeming to pray at what, to the outsider, would appear to be two separate religious institutions and in two different religious traditions.

Indeed, shrines and temples offer many similar forms of lucky charms and prayers for similar motivations, while some important festival occasions in the year (such as the New Year festival) may be celebrated at both shrines and temples alike. Often, too, despite there being official and doctrinally-ordained patterns of worship that distinguish Buddhist from Shinto institutions, ordinary people very often do not observe (and might not be aware of) those differences.

In other areas, too, the two religions have displayed complementary orientations, seen most clearly in the ways that the two fit into Japanese life-cycle patterns. As we have seen, Shinto's myths are particularly concerned with beginnings, and with the avoidance of death as a taboo subject, while Buddhism offers explanations of death and provides ritual procedures to deal with it. In such terms the two traditions have fitted together within the framework of social and life-cycle rituals that religions often cater for. Shinto has been largely concerned with beginnings, its *kami* serving as guardians over the young and growing, with a series of life-cycle rituals, such as the *hatsumiyamairi* or first shrine visit, when the new baby is taken to a shrine, given a blessing, and placed under the protection of the *kami*, while Buddhism is the vehicle, in Japan, for funerals and dealing with death.

This division of labour, as it were, between the two concerning the beginning and end of life has been an important element, enabling the two traditions to coexist to the extent that they have done, right up to the present day. This is not to say that neither tradition deals with the other's area of speciality. Buddhist temples do perform blessings for new babies, and Shinto funerals are not wholly unknown, occurring for members of the Imperial family and

Shinto priests and their families. However, they are rare, and the dissociation between Shinto and death remains one of the religion's most marked features.

In normal terms, what this all points to is a high level of interaction within the lives of the Japanese, who use both religious traditions together, and for whom both are intertwining parts of a common religious culture, rather than conflicting and competing traditions. This interaction may be seen also in the fact that many Japanese households have both a *butsudan*, a family Buddhist altar, enshrining the memorial tablets of its ancestors, the dead of the household, as well as a *kamidana* or Shinto altar, which enshrines local protective or household *kami*.

There is no sense that in praying to both of these sets of figures one is engaging in any form of contradictory behaviour, for it is a general characteristic of the Japanese religious world that people can use two or more religious traditions together and that they need not face the type of 'either-or' choice of affiliation that is normal in many other cultures. This pattern has developed through the centuries-old interaction between Shinto and Buddhism at grassroots levels, in which each has helped empower the other, and in which its deities have intertwined, frequently working together and cultivating complementary areas of concern.

As such, when, in later chapters, we look at some of the popular activities that occur at Shinto shrines, we need to be aware that many of these may also occur in very similar forms, perhaps even performed by the same people, in Buddhist settings as well.

Chapter 4

Shinto Shrines

Shinto, as we have seen, is not a coordinated, single tradition and it does not have a single, organized structure with a defined leader or spiritual head. The most important single organization for Shinto shrines is the Jinja Honchō, whose teachings particularly revolve around the view that the *kami* (who include the spirits of the ancestors) provide or have provided the living with the benefits and blessings of abundant life, and that therefore it is a human duty to express gratitude to, and venerate, the *kami*.

The performance of such rituals of veneration should be conducted in a spirit of sincerity, cheerfulness and purity: all three of these characteristics are highly valued attributes and moral qualities in Shinto. Jinja Honchō's Shinto teachings also stress that one should help and assist others without expectation of reward, and that all should strive for the attainment of peace and prosperity for Japan and for the world.

⊙ *Inner shrine, Ise*

However, while Jinja Honchō to some degree represents the Shinto mainstream, it does not have jurisdiction over all Shinto shrines or have the capacity to issue doctrinal or other injunctions that are binding on them all. Moreover, many important shrines are not associated with it, such as Fushimi Inari shrine, in Kyoto. Nor do all Shinto shrine lineages focus on Ise: for example, Izumo shrine in Shimane prefecture has it own lineage of dependent shrines and is an alternative source of authority and leadership within Shinto.

⊙ *Sacred tree with ropes* (shimenawa) *and paper strips* (gohei)

Even where they are affiliated to a broader organization, local shrines retain much independence, for each shrine has its own traditions, legends, rituals and practices relating to local circumstance and history. In general terms, however, they share a number of common characteristics through which many of the chief themes and the essences of Shinto may be expressed and experienced. If the concept of *kami* is central to the nature of Shinto, so too are its shrines, for it is at these locations that the *kami* are believed to be present, and it is at them that the important events – the rituals and festivals, and the practices of praying to and worshipping the *kami* – primarily take place.

Types and Structures of Shrines

Shrines are locations and institutions which formally mark the presence of a *kami* (or, more commonly, of a number of *kami*). There are various terms used in Japanese to denote a shrine, the most common being *jinja*, which simply means the shrine of a *kami*. A shrine can involve huge and complex structures, consisting of hundreds of buildings and sub-shrines, gathered around one or more central halls of worship and covering large tracts of land. Fushimi Inari shrine, for example, covers a whole mountain area in southern Kyoto, and contains several thousands of *torii* and subshrines known as *otsuka* (sacred stone mounds at which people worship). Yet they can also be minuscule structures, sometimes little more than a foot or so high and containing minute ornaments and a tiny altar.

Shrines operate on a number of different levels: major shrines such as Meiji shrine, the Ise shrines or Fushimi Inari have a national clientele, and may have large numbers of religious associations known as *kō* affiliated to them from across the country, receiving millions of worshippers at major festivals, and sometimes being the focus of mass pilgrimages. More commonly, though, shrines cater to their local communities, and their *kami* serve as guardian deities for the area and community around them.

Traditionally, all households in the area of such shrines would be affiliated to it, and residents regarded as *ujiko*, a term literally meaning 'child of the clan' but in reality equivalent to parishioner. Local households would thus incur obligations to the shrine, in terms of donations for its upkeep and assistance in preparing for its festivals, and would be expected to worship periodically at it. In modern times, this system has greatly eroded, and although it continues to some degree in more rural areas, in many urban and newly developed areas it may not exist at all.

Signs of the Sacred

Shrines do not have to be buildings. Since Shinto views the presence of *kami* as inherent in the natural world, any place is potentially the abode of a *kami* and is thus potentially the location of a shrine. Trees, rocks and other natural objects may in themselves mark the presence of or be the abodes of *kami*, and they can therefore serve as shrines without the need for special buildings. Some mountains (for example, Mount Miwa near Nara, the location of Miwa shrine) are regarded as the object of worship in themselves and the shrines on them have no specific hall of worship where the *kami* is believed to dwell: the mountain itself is that sanctuary.

What is common to shrines is the notion that they are sacred places where *kami* reside and which are empowered by the *kami*. They are places where the *kami* may be worshipped and where interactions between the realities of humans and of the *kami* may occur. A shrine thus occupies an area sanctified (usually as a result of a myth or foundation legend) by the presence of one or more *kami*, and it is normally marked out as such by symbols of the sacred, most commonly the *torii*, which acts as a boundary marker between the sacred space inhabited by the *kami* and the ordinary world around it.

Shrines are often surrounded by a grove of trees, and may be close to a stream, or at the foot of a mountain, with their locations and surroundings thus reminding one of the close associations posited between Shinto and the natural world.

» *Shimenawa* – Sacred Rope

Another common marker of the presence of the *kami* is the *shimenawa*, or sacred rope, which is normally made of straw and, hung with strips of cloth or paper, indicates the presence of a *kami* and of sacred locations. *Shimenawa* are often tied around trees and rocks to signify their sanctity, and they may be hung also from *torii* or across the front of shrine buildings. Perhaps the most famous *shimenawa* in Japan, and almost certainly the largest and thickest, are those at the Izumo shrine in Shimane.

Shrines usually have protective guardians posted at their gates to ward off evil spirits and bad luck. One of the most common forms of guardian is a pair of *komainu* or Korean dogs, fierce lion-like canines, which may sit at either side of the entry; another is a pair of demon kings known as *niō*, which are commonly found at Buddhist temples but sometimes also at Shinto shrines.

Since purity is a cardinal virtue in Shinto and it is believed that the *kami* will be offended if one approaches them in an impure state, it is normal when visiting shrines to engage in some form of purification process. Merely passing through the *torii* and past the ferocious gaze of the guardians may be enough to drive away impure thoughts, but it is common also to make some physical gesture towards purity as well, and thus, inside the entrance to a shrine one will find a *temizuya* (water fountain) where worshippers can rinse their mouths and hands in a simple act of purification. At some shrines (the Inner shrine at Ise is a good example) one might have to cross a bridge across a stream or river in order to approach the main shrine, and this act of crossing sacred water also serves as a purification activity.

Shrine Buildings and Inner Sanctuaries

Generally the most important building in any shrine complex is the *honden* or main hall of worship, which is approached from the main gate along a path known as the *sandō*. At the back of the honden there is an inner sanctum containing a sacred object known as a *shintai* (literally, the body of the *kami*) which marks the presence of the main figure of worship at the shrine, and in which its spirit is normally believed to reside.

Mirrors are often used as *shintai* (as, for example, with the sacred symbol of Amaterasu at Ise) because they symbolize many of the qualities affirmed in Shinto ideals: they are pure and reflective, radiating light and reflecting the pure nature of the *kami*. *Kami* are almost never depicted in physical form as statues.

Before the inner sanctuary is an altar at which offerings are made to the *kami*, usually by the shrine priest, and on which a sacred wand known as a *gohei* is placed. This is made up of a series of white paper strips and it signifies that the *kami* is present in the inner sanctum.

Since the *honden* is the location where offerings and prayers are made to the *kami* it usually has

❱ Important Shrines and Locations

DAZAIFU TENMANGŪ – at Dazaifu in Kyūshū, near the city of Fukuoka, this is the original shrine dedicated to the spirit of Sugawara no Michizane, and one of the main shrines dedicated to the *kami* of education, Tenjin, in Japan, with branch shrines throughout the country. Tenman is another name for Tenjin.

FUSHIMI INARI TAISHA – the most important of the 30,000 or more shrines dedicated to Inari, this is in southern Kyoto.

ISE JINGŪ – perhaps the most sacred of all shrines in Japan: in fact the Ise shrines consist of two shrines in the town of Ise in the Kii peninsula: the Naikū (Inner Shrine) and Gekū (Outer Shrine). The chief *kami* at the Inner Shrine is Amaterasu.

ISHIKIRI SHRINE, OSAKA – a popular shrine of healing which gets millions of visitors each year praying to the Ishikiri gods because of their reputed powers of healing.

IWASHIMIZU HACHIMANGŪ – important shrine dedicated to Hachiman, in the town of Yawata near Kyoto: this shrine has close associations with the Imperial household, and is also a guardian protector shrine of the city of Kyoto.

IZUMO TAISHA – dedicated to Okuninushi no Mikoto, a *kami* with special powers relating to love and marriage, at Izumo in Shimane prefecture.

JISHU SHRINE – in Kyoto, just next to the famous Buddhist temple Kiyomizudera, this small shrine is widely known for its *kami*'s powers relating to love and marriage, and is a popular destination of young lovers and couples.

KASUGA TAISHA – in Nara. formerly the Fujiwara clan shrine, it becama a major regional shrine and developed an association with Kōfukuji, a Buddhist temple in Nara.

KITANO TENMANGŪ – in Kyoto, this is the shrine established in the then capital to appease the spirit of Sugawara no Michizane, who became the deity of learning Tenjin: it remains an immensely popular shrine for aspiring scholars and for students seeking divine support when they take their examinations.

KOTOHIRAGŪ (KOTOHIRA SHRINE) – popularly known as Konpira-san, this shrine at Kotohira in Kagawa prefecture on the island of Shikoku commands views across to the Inland Sea and enshrines the deity Konpira. It is especially popular among those who make a living from the sea (e.g. sailors, shipbuilders, fishermen) and is famed for its *emadō* (hall of votive tablets).

MEIJI JINGŪ – dedicated to the spirit of the former Emperor Meiji, in the heart of Tokyo: the most visited shrine in Japan during the New Year's festival.

NISHINOMIYA EBISŪ – major shrine to the *kami* Ebisu, at Nishinomiya, halfway between Osaka and Kobe: its *hatsu Ebisu* (first Ebisu shrine visit of the year) festival on 9–10 January each year attracts hundreds of thousands of shopkeepers and people running small businesses seeking Ebisu's support in the coming year.

SUMIYOSHI TAISHA, OSAKA – the Sumiyoshi *kami* were amongst those produced after Izanagi's ritual purification, and are popular as guarantors of marine safety and as gods of business. The Sumiyoshi shrine is one of the most popular of all shrines in Osaka, Japan's second city, and is its main venue for worship at the New Year period.

TSURUOKA HACHIMANGŪ – at Kamakura, near Tokyo: another major Hachiman shrine which attracts visitors from all over Japan, but especially from the Tokyo region.

YUTOKU INARI – important shrine in Kyūshū, in southern Japan, dedicated to Inari: one of the leading Inari shrines in Japan.

space inside it for this purpose; often access to the interior of the *honden* is restricted only to priests and shrine officiants, and perhaps occasionally participants in special prayer rituals. Offerings to the *kami*, apart from monetary ones, are usually placed in the *honden* or on the altar. These may range from foodstuffs and, especially at harvest time, the fruits of agricultural labour, to all manner of other goods.

At the annual festival of a shrine close to where I used to live in Japan the local shopkeepers made donations to the shrine relating to their businesses, and accompanied by prayers seeking the *kami's* assistance and benediction. Thus the local rice merchants would offer rice, the saké merchant bottles of saké, and so on: one year I noted a brand new bicycle placed before the altar, the offering from the local bicycle shop.

⊙ *Shinto priests (including female, centre) carrying a shaku (mace)*

Normal worship is performed from outside, at the front of the hall, where one also finds a box for offerings (*saisen bako*) into which petitioners throw some coins before clapping their hands twice (the standard means of alerting the *kami* of one's presence), bowing their heads and praying. Often a bell hangs in front of the *honden*, and worshippers can also summon the attention of the *kami* by pulling on its bellrope.

Around the *honden* are often grouped numerous smaller shrines and sub-shrines each enshrining one or more *kami*. While this is especially so at larger shrines, even small ones may have a number of subsidiary shrine buildings. The *kami* enshrined in them are also, like the *kami* at the *honden*, normally resident at the location, but there is at least one prominent and famed exception to this. This is found in the popular beliefs relating to the Izumo shrine in Shimane prefecture. Its main *kami*, Okuninushi no Mikoto, is famed for its skills in aiding people to find love and for the power of *enmusubi*, joining people together in love and marriage.

Shrines are usually simple in form, and are built using natural materials such as cypress wood, often roofed with layers of cypress bark. Many traditional shrines are rebuilt on a regular cyclical basis, as is the case at Ise, where the main shrines are rebuilt every twenty years, always in the same style as before, which dates back to the seventh century CE. Only natural materials are used in the rebuilding, and they come from all over Japan. The process of rebuilding thus symbolizes the importance of renewal and regeneration in Shinto, as well as the

» October 'Meeting of *Kami*'

According to legend, all the *kami* of Japan congregate at Izumo during the month of October to discuss such matters as love and marriage, and hence at this time they leave their normal sanctuaries to reside at Izumo. This month is known as *kamiari tsuki* (the month when the *kami* are present) at Izumo, and *kanna zuki* (the month when the *kami* are absent) elsewhere. Around the main shrine at Izumo are rows of sub-shrines that accommodate the *kami* from the rest of Japan at this time.

maintenance of tradition and the national stature of the shrine.

However, the process of building and maintaining shrines using only natural and traditional materials is extremely costly: such buildings are also difficult to maintain, and because they are made of wood, are liable to fires and other such disasters. As a result, it is increasingly common for new shrines to be built out of concrete and other such materials, that are more in tune with modern building methods and styles.

Shrine Animals

Often within the shrine one will see statues of animals, for many *kami* have animal attendants or messengers who are believed to communicate with and protect them. The most common of these are the fox statues found at Inari shrines which are so prevalent and so closely identified with Inari that Inari is sometimes described, wrongly, as the fox god: in fact the fox is a messenger of Inari, not the *kami* itself.

Another animal presence found especially at large shrines is the horse, which is in mythical terms both a messenger and mount of the *kami*. Horses play a part in many important Shinto rituals, when they symbolically bear the *kami* in procession or are paraded during rituals to symbolize the presence of the *kami*.

Shrines which keep horses for this purpose include the Ise shrines and the Iwashimizu Hachiman shrine at Yawata south of Kyoto, an ancient shrine with close links to the Imperial family, which is regarded as a guardian shrine of Kyoto. Since keeping horses is an expensive business, however, many shrines prefer not to follow this custom, while others, such as the Izumo shrine and the Fushimi Inari shrine, have opted for a more pragmatic solution: they keep fullsize model horses!

Shrine Officiants

The chief officiants at Shinto shrines are priests, who are normally, although not exclusively, male. The standard terms for a Shinto priest are *kannushi* or *shinshoku*, but the priesthood is divided into a number of ranks, which relate both to the status of the shrine itself and their position within it. Larger shrines might employ several priests, while smaller ones may only have a part-time priest or none at all: many shrines, especially in rural areas, no longer are able to support a priest economically, and may be taken care of by concerned local residents or community associations. The chief priest of a shrine holds the rank of *gūji*: other ranks below this include *gongūji* (deputy chief priest) and *negi*.

The role of priest is often hereditary, especially at many of the major shrines, but it also requires, in the present day, formal training and qualifications. These are obtained both through training at the shrines themselves, where trainee priests may learn how to perform specific rituals and how to organize and manage financial affairs, and through attendance at one of the two Shinto universities (Kokugakuin University in Tokyo or Kōgakkan University at Ise) in Japan, which have seminaries for training priests.

When performing their priestly roles they normally wear flowing robes (a *kimono* and a *hakama* or divided skirt, often with an outer robe as well) that are based on those of the Heian (794–1185) period court nobles. They also wear a hat, either an *eboshi* which is a simple cap-like affair, or a *kanmuri*, a tall, ceremonial hat worn in formal rituals, and black lacquered wooden shoes, and carry, as a symbol of office and authority, a black wooden mace known as a *shaku*.

The role of the priest centres on the shrine and its maintenance both in practical and spiritual terms. Besides overseeing the running of the shrine, ministering to its parishioners and catering to those who wish to worship and make requests to the *kami*, the priest has a primary role in caring for and honouring the *kami*. It is the priests who may enter the inner sanctum of shrines and approach the *kami* directly (in many shrines, only the priest can perform this role) and it is they who serve as mediators between the people and the *kami*, relaying the requests and offerings of the former to the latter.

Priests also perform the rites of transference when the *kami* are moved into the temporary shrines known as *mikoshi*, which are carried during festivals, sanctify new shrines or altars through the transference of the spiritual essence of the *kami* to them, and officiate at numerous rituals both in and outside the shrine.

Although priests are the primary officiants at rituals and festive events, they do not always play the most immediately active role in them. This role is frequently performed by *miko*, shrine maidens, who also play an important role in the running of shrines. *Miko* in earlier times were often considered as spirit mediums with shamanic powers, through whom the *kami* might transmit oracles and messages for the benefit of the community, but this function is rarely found in the present day. More commonly nowadays, shrine maidens help run shrine offices, selling the various amulets and talismans that are available there, looking after shrine visitors, and serving as officiants in shrine rituals. They are normally young women who may be full-time servants of the shrine, although frequently part-time. Sometimes the unmarried daughter of the priest fills this role. Larger shrines may employ a number of *miko*, and many also, at major festival times, hire extra help to perform these roles. *Miko* usually wear a white upper robe and a red *hakama* or divided skirt, although in some solemn rites they may be clothed in white, a colour signifying purity in Shinto.

Chapter 5

Life-Cycles, Festivals & Rituals

While many Japanese people may have a relationship with a local community shrine and visit it regularly, the predominant patterns of shrine visiting and *kami* worship are more irregular and related to special needs and occasions such as festivals and calendrical and life-cycle rituals.

The yearly round of festivals and ritual events (*nenjū gyōji*) mentioned in the Introduction forms an important aspect of shrine calendars (and also of Buddhist temple calendars). Such cyclical events, which were traditionally associated with the passing of the seasons and the agricultural cycle, in former times provided a temporal framework for the lives of people and communities in Japan, especially in rural areas that depended on agricultural modes of existence. Shinto festivals and rituals also helped frame the individual and familial life-cycles as well, with various rituals associated with different stages of life.

Although the patterns of life have changed drastically in modern Japan, with the shift from a rural agricultural society to an industrial technological and predominantly urban one, the traditional calendar of festivals has continued to

⊙ *An arrow for good luck at New Year*

frame the Japanese year. Major holidays, for example, are largely based on the old ritual/festive calendar, while important dates and events in the annual religious calendar continue to attract large numbers of participants. Important stages in the lives of individuals also continue to be marked out by religious observances at shrines.

There is an inherently festive aspect to the cycle of ritual events. The calendrical cycle and the individual's life cycle provide numerous occasions for celebrating or marking out stages of transition, fruition and growth, as well as for guarding against unforeseen problems, and for harnessing the support of the *kami* in the course of community and individual activities. It would be impossible to list all the various occasions which provide scope for ritual or festive activity, and here only a select few occasions and events will be mentioned. The importance of beginnings, which is emphasized in myths, comes through clearly in Shinto calendrical cycles, with many important festivals associated with beginnings, such as the New Year festival, and the various festivals associated with the first agricultural activities of the yearly cycle, and with planting the crops. In the life cycle, too, important occasions when one seeks the blessing of the *kami* are especially associated with the earlier years of life and of growing, a time when the support of the *kami* is especially needed.

Among the most important festive and commemorative occasions in the individual life cycle are the first shrine visit *hatsumiyamairi* for new babies, and the *shichigosan* (7–5–3) festival in November for young children; other life-cycle rituals that many undertake are connected to the notion that certain stages of life are unlucky or fraught with difficulty – a concept known in Japan as *yakudoshi* or unlucky years – and at which it is wise to receive special blessings from the gods and perform special rituals to acquire their protection.

Yearly Cycle of Events

In the yearly cycle of events, some festive
occasions are followed throughout the country,
while others are limited to particular regions or
shrines. The New Year's festival is the largest of
all, the occasion for the large majority of Japanese
people to visit Shinto shrines to pay their respects
to the gods and to ask their protection and
favours in the coming year. It is also an occasion
when they like to delve into what the future may
hold: at this time in particular it is common for
people to acquire *omikuji*, divination slips or
oracle lots, which are read, usually with some
amusement, and then tied up at the shrine.

The New Year's festival contains numerous
motifs for eradicating the misfortunes of the past,
of transition, renewal and looking forward to the
future. It is also a collective occasion, when
people gather together in family groups or with
close friends, share a special family meal (on the
evening of 31 December) and perform the round
of shrine visiting together as a family group, or
with their close friends.

The act of performing the first shrine visit, or
hatsumôde, is also a communal and collective
event: people visiting their local shrine at this time
can feel part of their local communities, and may
indeed find themselves crowded into the shrine
courtyard with their neighbours and other members
of their local community. The event has similar
effects on a wider, national level, for all over Japan

❯❯ Important Life-Cycle Rituals and Festivals

hatsumiyamairi – first shrine visit in which newborn babies are taken to the shrine (traditionally, the local shrine, but often in the modern day a large and famous one) to be blessed, placed under the protection of the *kami* and become accepted as a parishioner of the shrine and hence a member of the local community. The baby is normally carried by its grandmother, and the ritual is supposed to occur approximately thirty days after birth.

shichigosan – literally, 7–5–3 festival: a further stage in the process of bonding the growing child with the *kami*, in which boys aged five and girls aged seven and three are taken to the shrine and blessed. The official date of the festival is 15 November, but at popular shrines *shichigosan* may be celebrated throughout the month, with the Sunday nearest 15 November being the peak day. The children are dressed brightly – usually a colourful kimono for the girls – and are accompanied by their parents.

yakudoshi – literaly 'unlucky years':In the cyclical and divinatory patterns inherited from Taoism, certain ages were considered to be inauspicious and fraught with danger, and as a result it was customary for people of these years (the most inauspicious being 33 for women and 42 for men) to make special shrine and temple visits at this time and perform various rituals and get protective amulets to ward off the danger. This custom is still widely followed in the present day, and shrines and temples specialising in *yakuyoke* (prevention of bad luck) perform special purification rituals for this purpose.

⊗ *Young men of the Kudan district (Tokyo) parading the local shrine
(omikoshi) during the summer festival*

the same performance is going on; at major shrines
the crowds may run into millions, and whether
joining in such crowds or participating on a smaller,
more local, scale, it is not difficult for *hatsumōde*
worshippers to sense that they are engaging in an
event along with their fellow citizens. As such, the
festival has a powerful communal aspect that
enforces and emphasizes a sense of collective
Japanese identity.

The New Year's festival heralds the coming of a
new cycle of festive events that run throughout the
year and that are often linked to seasonal changes

and agricultural patterns. They include the beckoning of spring, and the concomitant symbolic driving away of the cold weather, in the *setsubun* festival of February (an occasion when ritual officiants symbolically also drive away evil and beckon good fortune), and agricultural festivals welcoming the beginnings of the new agricultural cycle in spring: April, in particular, is a month with many festivals, including various *ta-uesai* or rice planting festivals.

The heat of summer is punctuated by numerous summer festivals (*natsu matsuri*) whose theme is generally associated with protection, summer being the time when the crops grow but are most vulnerable, whether to bad weather conditions (drought or excessive rain) or insects. Because the summer is hot and wet, too, it breeds illnesses, and many festivals of summer were originally associated with the eradication of pestilences, such as the Gion *matsuri* in Kyoto.

Autumn brings another round of festivals mostly connected with the celebration of the harvest, while the months before the end of year bring various other festivals, including the *shichogosan* festival of November.

Festivals: *Matsuri*

The Japanese word *matsuri*, which is normally translated as festival, contains meanings of celebration, festivity, ritual, veneration and prayer: in essence, a *matsuri* is a combination of all these, sometimes with an emphasis on some of the more solemn of these, at others with a greater emphasis on the more celebratory, and frequently combining aspects of both.

Basically, *matsuri* give thanks to the *kami* for their support and benevolence, and venerate, honour and please them so that they will continue with this support. They are also important as occasions that provide the community and people in general with an opportunity to escape from the normal constrictions of everyday life, to let off steam, celebrate and enjoy themselves: just as the holy days or festive days in the European Christian calendar were originally the only occasions and opportunities for 'holidays' (the original meaning of the word derives from holy days), so too were *matsuri* in pre-modern Japan the prime chance ordinary people had to relax and enjoy themselves. This link of religion, relaxation and escaping from the everyday patterns of life has not disappeared but continues to be part of the present structure of *matsuri*.

Festivals may be wild and exuberant, involving dancing, crowds, drinking, and the like. The *hadaka matsuri* or 'naked' festivals that occur in many places in the depths of winter, involve young men clad in loincloths and participating in competitive actions, striving to show off their strength, and simultaneously demonstrating their defiance of the cold and of the gloom of winter through their virtual nudity.

A prominent feature in many festivals is the removal of the shrine *kami* to an alternative location or temporary shrine where they are accorded special veneration during the festive period. The journey to that special temporary shrine is done in a *mikoshi* or portable shrine, into which a shrine *kami* is ritually transferred and then carried in procession to the new resting place.

The procession may be a raucous affair, the *mikoshi* carried in turn by different groups of men, with each group representing the people of a particular ward covered by the shrine or the areas through which the *mikoshi* passes. Often the carriers drink liberally and shout rhythmically as they carry the portable shrine, and the procession thus becomes increasingly wild and noisy the longer it continues.

The *mikoshi* will be brought to a halt outside the houses of families who have been prominent patrons of the shrine, and a special ritual celebration and blessing will occur there: it is also rumoured that, in some festivals, households contribute financially to the shrine and festival for fear that if they do not the *mikoshi* may 'accidentally' bump against their property and cause it damage.

Carrying the *mikoshi* has an important symbolic meaning, too. Because they are usually heavy and cumbersome, they can only be successfully carried and guided through the streets by a group of people working closely together, and pulling in the same direction – the same things needed for successful agricultural work, for good cooperative community activities, and, indeed, for cooperative economic and social life in general.

The festival may involve colourful processions that accompany the *mikoshi* with much noise and pageantry, and that are vast visual spectacles attracting huge crowds and incorporating a strong tourist dimension. Markets and stalls offering food, drinks, souvenirs, and much else besides, often line the routes of festive processions and may be set up also in shrine courtyards for the occasion, and festivals can thus be occasions of great economic activity.

» Tanabata Festival, Sendai

Many of the large festivals of Japan, such as the Tanabata Festival of Sendai, held in early July, have become huge tourist attractions that are important elements in their location's economy. Sendai's Tanabata Festival, for instance, brings as many as two million people into the city each year, to watch the spectacle, participate, and of course to spend their money.

Not all festivals, however, are wild, noisy or even commercially oriented: many display a serious, austere, and ritually refined aspect, in which participants demonstrate their awe and respect for the *kami*. The annual festival at the Iwashimizu Hachiman shrine is such an example. It starts around midnight on the morning of 15 September each year, and replicates the form of the festival as it was when it first began in the ninth century.

In this festival the *kami* is taken out of the main shrine in a *mikoshi*, and carried in a slow, formal and atmospherically solemn procession down the steep path of the shrine (which sits atop a hillside) to a shrine at the foot of the hill, at which a series of formal rituals honouring the *kami* occur. The procession accompanying the *mikoshi* is made up of people (including young children) dressed in the clothes of the Heian period, and thus mirrors the Heian era Iwashimizu shrine festival; it is also accompanied by musicians who play the slow, melodious shrine music known as *gagaku*. The whole festival occurs at night, and as the *mikoshi* is first brought out of the main shrine, carried by priests in ancient Japanese robes, the night lit only by the flickering light of oil lamps, and the air rent by the mournfully haunting sounds of the reed instruments used in *gagaku* (see illus. p. 121), it is understandable how onlookers and worshippers can be struck by a sense of awe, and how, in the midst of such ritual and festive solemnity, many think they can feel the presence of the *kami*.

Shinto Rituals

Rituals and ceremonies are core activities at shrines, and are vital and central elements in festivals, even the wildest and most joyous of which may contain solemn and austere ceremonies in which relationships are established and intensified between *kami* and the human realms. The aims of rituals are multiple, but in general terms they include acquiring the help of the *kami* in preventing bad luck and bringing good, honouring and worshipping the *kami* and expressing gratitude for benefits granted, and creating a sense of unity and communion between *kami* and people.

Through rituals many of the main tenets of Shinto, such as the emphasis on purity and the importance of venerating and maintaining harmony with the *kami*, are expressed, as are many key elements in Shinto's underlying mythology.

Rituals are conducted normally under the auspices of the priests, although often the shrine maiden plays a central role as well. Shinto rituals and ceremonies commonly involve four aspects and stages: purification, offerings and worship, supplication and prayer, and communion or feast. Taken as a whole, the ritual procedure thus involves preparations that make the participants ready to meet and communicate with the *kami*, means for engaging the attention and benevolence of the *kami*, procedures for placing requests and wishes before the *kami*, and a closure of the process through communal feasting.

Purification, as we have seen, is a critical activity, emphasized in myths as essential for removing evils and as a means of bringing about renewal. Prior to important shrine rituals the participants such as priests and *miko* are expected to undergo some purification processes which might involve ritual bathing, donning clean robes, and perhaps a period of abstinence, for example, from certain foods such as meat. Ritual bathing is termed *misogi*, a practice that can vary from the simple hand-washing at the *temizuya* to forms of asceticism, with the priests pouring large amounts of cold water over themselves or immersing themselves in the waters of a river or standing under a waterfall.

The purification process in general is known as *harai* or *harae* (the terms are interchangeable, and may also be written with the honrofic 'o' before them, as in *o-harai*). A number of elements are commonly used in the rituals of purification: water, of course, is commonly used, but so, too, is salt, which may be sprinkled over ritual participants or over the ritual area. Salt is also used as an agent of purification in the rituals of Sumō wrestling, which have close associations with Shinto ritual: before fighting, the wrestlers toss handfuls of salt into the ring to purify it and drive off bad luck, and if any blood is shed in a fight, the ring is immediately purified with salt.

Other means of purification involve blessing the participants by waving a purification wand (*harai-gushi*) over their heads to symbolically sweep away bad spirits and misfortune. As part of their ritual uniform, *miko* carry a cluster of bells known as a *suzu* and these also may be used in symbolic purification rites, being waved over the heads of worshippers to bless them and eradicate spiritual impurities.

Besides proffering physical objects, another important way of making offerings to the *kami* is to entertain them. This is a role normally performed by the *miko*, most commonly through the sacred ritual dance known as *kagura*, a term that means 'entertaining the *kami*', and that symbolically harks back to the sexually provocative actions of the female deity who danced before Amaterasu's cave and brought so much enjoyment to the other *kami*.

Praying to the *Kami*

Praying to the *kami* is an integral element in rituals as it is in individual worship. In rituals, the forms of prayer used to address the *kami* are known as *norito*. These are read by the priest, and are normally in classical Japanese (barely understood by most listeners). Their content varies from ritual to ritual, but commonly they will praise and honour the *kami* and articulate the wishes and requests to be placed before them. There are numerous collections of *norito*, the earliest being in the *Engishiki*, a collection of court records completed in 927 CE, which contains the texts of twenty-seven *norito* used at the time.

The final stage of rituals and ceremonies is the *naorai*, or sacred feast. This may simply involve each worshipper supping a small cup of saké that has been offered to the *kami* earlier, or it may be an elaborate feast for the participants and patrons of a ceremony. On such occasions the food may be of the highest class, and accompanied by copious quantities of saké.

Symbolically, the *kami* is present during the meal, for the inner meaning of *naorai* is to commune with the *kami* through the sharing of food. Thus, the meal is a form of communion with the *kami*, in which human relations are also affirmed through the process of sharing saké or a meal. *Naorai* is thus a celebration, both of the closing and completion of a ritual, and of the bonds that join humans together and link them to the *kami*, while it is equally an occasion for festivity. In its emphasis on communion and celebration it is a symbol of Shinto rituals and festivals in general.

Chapter 6

Prayers & Communications with the *Kami*

Turning to the Gods

Whether at rituals, festivals and other events in the Shinto calendar, or on visits conditioned by personal wishes, ranging from the regular visits of shrine faithful to the more sporadic visits by those needing to call on the *kami*'s help, Shinto shrines provide numerous means of interaction with the *kami*. In the previous chapter we looked at some of the more formal and organized means of interaction through such events as rituals and festivals, and in this chapter we will look at other, more informal means of interaction, with a special focus on the objects – the amulets, talismans and the like that one can purchase at shrines, and through which the presence of the *kami* may be manifest and their assistance sought.

Much shrine visiting and praying is need-based, rather than being conditional on faith or continuing association with particular shrines. Shinto is not a religious tradition that demands prior commitment before one makes petitions or prayers seeking the help of the *kami*. There is a popular phrase *kurushii toki no kamidanomi*, 'turning to the gods in times of

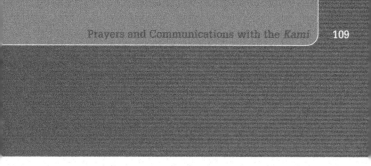

⊙ *Fox messenger figures at an Inari shrine*

trouble', which appropriately expresses the basic
sentiment that the *kami* are there to assist one, and
thus can be turned to whenever one is in need.

This aspect of Shinto activity is perhaps best
exemplified at the period before the annual school
and university entrance examinations in January
and February each year. At this time shrines across
Japan, and particularly those associated with
Tenjin, are crowded with young people writing
petitions and making prayers to the *kami* to enable
them to pass their examinations.

It is a fair assumption that the vast majority of
these young people are not constant worshippers at

such shrines, are probably not particularly driven by religious sentiments, may normally state that they are not religious, and may even normally express intellectual disbelief in the existence of *kami*. Yet, faced with the stress and worries of examinations that are crucial to their future, the vast majority, even though they know they have worked and studied hard, are liable to turn to the *kami* and seek their support.

This process, which serves to emotionally reassure and calm the petitioner, also recognizes the uncertainties of chance. No matter how much one might prepare for an event, one cannot eliminate the

⊙ *Offerings to the* kami, *including saké and rice*

vagaries of chance, and in such terms humans will always be fallible and in need of reassurance and help from elsewhere. It is in such areas, and at such times, that the *kami* may be called upon, and Shinto thoughts affirming the reliance of humans on the assistance of the *kami* are thus expressed through the actions of the petitioners.

Sincerity and Gratitude

'Turning to the gods' and petitioning for assistance necessitate treating the *kami* with proper respect and following correct ways of behaviour towards them. In simple terms this means approaching the *kami* in a pure state of mind and demonstrating such cardinal virtues affirmed by Shinto as sincerity and gratitude, while engaging in a reciprocal process of interaction with the shrine and its *kami*.

Sincerity and gratitude are interlinked: one should be sincere and pure in mind when one deals with the *kami*, and at the same time retain a sense of gratitude towards the *kami*. Gratitude is an important attribute for Shinto, and it is a basic injunction of Shinto that when one is praying to the *kami*, one should do so in a spirit of gratitude and thanks for their benevolence in providing the good things of life. Equally, petitioners should return to shrines to give thanks for favours granted – an obligation which, although not always followed, hints at the establishment of a continuing relationship between petitioner, shrine and *kami*.

Indeed, one Japanese study of the attitudes of

shrine visitors at Ishikiri shrine near Osaka, showed that a large number of them were regular visitors, whose prayers had been answered in the past by the shrine *kami*, and who had made return visits of thanks as a result, which had developed into a continuing practice. Naturally, Shinto shrines are keen to develop such regular patterns of visiting and prayer, for it helps create a stable clientele of the faithful, and their priests may therefore spend much energy on emphasizing the importance of gratitude.

In expressing their gratitude and sincerity petitioners are in effect trying to demonstrate their worthiness to receive assistance and benefits from the *kami*. They may do this in many ways, such as, for example, undergoing some ascetic feat when visiting a shrine. The *hyakudo mairi* (one hundred times circumambulation) practice seen at some shrines, in which petitioners walk around two stones in the shrine courtyard one hundred times as a form of austerity, is one example of this. It is, for instance, a practice commonly followed at Ishikiri shrine.

They may also embark on a pilgrimage to a specific shrine: in former times, pilgrims would go on foot, but the influences of modernity and the increasing pressures of time have altered this. Nowadays, it is more common for the pilgrimage to be done by convenient means such as public transport or by car, but the underlying meaning of the special journey of pilgrimage – leaving one's everyday routines to visit a sacred place, perform an act of worship and seek the blessing and support of a *kami* – remains common. So do the tourist aspects of pilgrimage: in earlier times, pilgrimages were the only opportunity many people had for travel, and it was common to combine religious and tourist aims together, for visitors to both pray and to enjoy themselves, to see new places, purchase souvenirs and get away from their normal routines for a while – the essence, in fact, of tourism, yet closely connected to pilgrimage, and a common element also in the present day.

Other means of expressing sincerity might include receiving a ritual blessing from the shrine priests or *miko*, sponsoring a special prayer ritual, or praying earnestly and making a vow to the *kami* – perhaps involving the pledge of further religious action if one's petition is favourably received.

Objects and Their Meanings

It is common also to acquire some tangible means through which a special connection can be made between the petitioner, shrine and *kami*, and through which the prayers and requests of the petitioner may be given form. These come in many forms, the most common of which are *ema* (votive tablets), *omamori* and *fuda* (both of which can be translated as amulets or talismans), and *hamaya* (a sacred arrow, a popular lucky protective symbol usually acquired at New Year). They are purchased at shrines for a small sum, and either taken home or left at the shrine, either thereby bringing a part of the shrine and its presence away with one, or leaving some sign of one's presence at the shrine.

Ema

Ema are votive tablets, usually made of wood, that are purchased at shrines. The word *ema* itself is made up of two ideograms meaning, respectively, picture (*e*) and horse (*ma*) and refers to the ancient belief that horses were go-betweens between humans and the gods, and that if one wished to make a special request to the gods, one should present the gods with a horse as a gift. Since this was economically not feasible for most people, horse figurines made of pottery were used instead, and excavations of early shrines have found evidence of this custom as far back as the seventh century CE. Such figurines in turn were replaced by wooden plaques with a picture of a horse and a written wish (the first *ema*).

Over the centuries, the designs of *ema* have expanded beyond just pictures of horses, and have come to depict a range of highly diverse and colourful symbols and pictures, from representations of the year animals – the twelve animals that, in Japan, represent each year in a twelve-year cycle similar to the zodiac – to depictions of stories and legends associated with the shrine's origins or deities, to symbolic designs that reflect the intentions of petitioners.

A common design shows an *ema* with the word *gokaku*, to attain education success, on it and an arrow hitting a target – a fairly clear picture of the wishes of the petitioner. Because of their colourful designs, which vary from shrine to shrine, many people purchase *ema* at shrines and take them home as souvenirs, but the standard use of them is to use them as a means of relating one's wishes to the *kami*.

Ema have been described as 'letters to the gods', for petitioners write on them their requests, after which they will hang them up at a special place designated for this purpose in the shrine, while accompanying this with a short prayer.

⊙ *Statue of sacred horse, with* ema, *at Izumo shrine*

What people write on *ema* varies according to their needs and wishes. *Ema*-writing is especially popular among the young, and is one of the chief means through which they petition the *kami* prior to school and college entrance examinations. Such messages, in asking the *kami*'s help, will often specify the school or college the student wishes to enter.

At shrines whose *kami* are noted for their effectiveness in the realm of love, couples may write an *ema* together pledging their love to each other and asking the gods to help them maintain this, or asking for help in conceiving a child. Likewise, an individual might ask the gods for help in finding a good partner.

People seeking to give up bad habits may write *ema* seeking the *kami*'s assistance in this task. They may also be used for more lighthearted reasons, in connection with one's personal interests: the author has seen *ema* written by small children asking that their pocket money be increased, and by sports fans asking the *kami* to assist their favourite baseball team in winning a championship. Usually, people write their names and often their addresses on the *ema* as well.

Shrines will normally leave the *ema* hanging there for some time, periodically clearing out the racks to make space for new ones, and conducting a special ritual service in which the old *ema* are burnt as offerings to the *kami*.

Omamori and *Fuda*

While *ema* are normally left at the shrine, *omamori* and *fuda* are taken away from it. Both are believed to have both protective and fortune-opening attributes.

The word *omamori* comes from the verb *mamoru*, to protect, and refers in origin to a protective amulet designed to ward off dangers and troubles, but they can also be lucky charms that beckon good luck as well. They come in various shapes and forms, the most common of which are in the form of small brocade bags on which the type of benefit promised is usually written (sometimes with the name of the shrine as well). Inside the bag there is usually a slip of paper with a prayer on it. *Omamori* are generally considered to be personal and localized, protective of a person or area, and carried on or around a person. Traffic safety *omamori* are placed in a car, while children may have an *omamori* for safety or for education success affixed to their schoolbags.

Fuda (or *ofuda*: the 'o' is an honorific term) are similar to *omamori* in that they may be protective, warding off bad luck, or they may also beckon good luck. Usually a flat-shaped piece of wood inscribed with sacred inscriptions, with a sacred binding of paper, they serve to protect areas and specific spaces, or groups of people. Families and households might, for example, acquire *fuda* to protect the family against bad luck or to bring prosperity to the household. Normally they are placed in some special place in the house: if the family has a *kamidana* (Shinto altar) then they will be placed there. If not, it is common to place them in the *butsudan*, the family Buddhist altar for the ancestors.

Both *omamori* and *fuda* are considered to be representations and manifestations of the *kami*. They are blessed in shrine rituals, through which it is believed the spirit of the *kami* passes into them, thus transforming them from being an object made of wood or cloth, into a manifestation of the spirit of the *kami*. As such they are sacred, and should be treated with respect. According to belief, the *kami* manifest in the amulet may use its power to absorb or deflect any bad luck coming the owner's way, or to draw good fortune towards the owner(s).

Hamaya

The word *hamaya* means 'evil destroying arrow' and, as its name suggests, it comes in the form of an arrow, usually adorned with sacred symbols and inscriptions. *Hamaya* are, like *omamori* and *fuda*, sacralized and thus are considered to contain the spiritual essence and protective powers of the *kami*. Commonly purchased during the *hatsumōde* first shrine visit of the year, their purpose is to guard the home against bad fortune. As such they are taken home and placed in the house, normally in its northeastern corner, which is known in Japanese as the *kimon* ('devil's gate') and is, according to Japanese geomantic ideas derived originally from Taoism, the unluckiest direction, the one from which misfortune might be expected.

Symbolic Meanings

Since *omamori, fuda* and *hamaya* are considered to be manifestations of the spirit of the *kami*, they are meant to be treated as sacred; indeed, shrines often issue instructions with them suggesting that they should be the focus of prayers, for they are in effect a representation of the shrine and *kami* that is taken home by the petitioner. In reality, however, they are often purchased not just as sacred objects but also as souvenirs of shrine visits, and as gifts for friends and family.

People do not, as a rule, believe that the acquisition of a talisman or amulet will necessarily have the effect of bringing good fortune: the efficacy of these objects is found not in mechanical terms but symbolic ones. All these objects symbolically express an underlying theme of the Japanese religious world mentioned earlier in this chapter, relating to the fallibility of humanity and our need for reassurance, for help in dealing with the unknown, and to the basic Shinto premise that life is lived in cooperation with, and is hence in part dependent on, the *kami*.

Amulets, talismans and votive tablets are a means of expressing these ideas in a concrete form. They serve simultaneously as a form of emotional reassurance, and as a reminder to petitioners of their obligations: to purchase an amulet or the like is in effect to engage in a contract of cooperation and commitment with the *kami*.

Cyclicality

Although *fuda* and the like are believed to be manifestations of the *kami*'s essence, they are nevertheless considered to be finite in terms of efficacy. The normal period for which they are valid is one year, after which popular belief suggests that they have absorbed all the negative influences they can, and hence it is time to change them. The normal way of doing this is to take the old ones back to a shrine (or temple, for all these are also found at Buddhist institutions), and to purchase new ones.

This process of returning old sacred objects, and replacing them with new ones, is especially widely seen at the New Year festival, when it is common to see people coming to the shrine bringing with them bags of old sacred objects, especially *hamaya*, which they deposit at the shrine – and then departing, after having paid their respects to the *kami* and offered their prayers, carrying their new talismans and *hamaya* that symbolize their hopes and aspirations for the coming year.

The returned sacred objects are then disposed of by the shrines and temples in a ritual fire that is believed to remove any bad luck accruing to them. While such ritual burnings may occur periodically over the year, as and when large numbers of old amulets get returned, many shrines also conduct a special ritual fire festival shortly after the New Year festival for this purpose. At Iwashimizu Hachiman shrine in Yawata, for example, such a ritual takes place on 19 January each year, in which a huge mound of returned *hamaya* are ritually burnt by priests to the accompaniment of ritual invocations, sacred music, and *kagura* ritual dances performed by shrine maidens. This whole process, as such, thus depicts the importance of cyclicality, and of regeneration and renewal in Shinto, a process that is also, as we have seen, integral to the Shinto round of festivals and the calendrical cycle of events surrounding Shinto shrines.

⊙ *Gagaku musicians at Ise*

Chapter 7

Shinto, Nationalism & Yasukuni Shrine

Yasukuni Shrine

The Yasukuni shrine is located at Kudanshita in central Tokyo, and while the shrine may not appear especially impressive in architectural terms, it and its surroundings seem to offer some quiet and respite from the hustle of the Tokyo streets. Indeed, the name of the shrine itself underlines such images of peace and tranquillity for Yasukuni means 'pacifying the country'.

The unknowing visitor dropping into the shrine to escape from the crowded streets for a short while, and enticed by the images of tranquillity conjured up by the name and the situation, would probably find it hard to imagine that this is the most contested and controversial religious space in post-war Japan, the focus of political disputes which have involved countless wranglings in the Japanese Parliament, and at times bitter protests from many religious groups in Japan as well as from Japan's Asian neighbours.

The controversies are rooted in the complex relationship between religion, politics and the state in earlier periods of Japanese history, which we

⊙ *Yasukuni shrine, Tokyo*

alluded to in Chapter Three. The great religious traditions of Japan, both Buddhism and Shinto, have at different times been pillars of the state, as shown by the position of Tōdaiji in Nara times, or Buddhism in the Tokugawa period. In modern times, as we saw earlier, Shinto played this role in the period from 1868 until Japan was defeated at the end of the war in 1945.

After the war, as we have seen, the Occupation government inaugurated a new democratic constitution which guaranteed religious freedom, affirmed the separation of religion and state, and forbade the state from using public funds for religious purposes. In addition, the Emperor (Hirohito, who died in 1989 after a reign of sixty-three years) renounced his divinity in a broadcast in 1946, thereby removing one of the main planks of pre-war State Shinto ideology.

The constitutional aims of providing Japan with the means to develop as a modern secular state were also intended to remove any possibility of a revival of the links between reverence for the Emperor as a deity, and the rampant nationalism and the state-controlled religion which, before the war, had been instrumental in suppressing religious freedoms and in creating the fascist state that waged war through much of Asia. While welcomed by large sectors of the population, the severing of the bonds of state and religion, and the changes in the status of the Emperor, have not been accepted by all, and there remains a lobby – consisting particularly of right-wing and con-servative nationalists, as well as various Shinto organizations, priests and adherents – that wishes to restore the links between government and religion, and to provide state support for Shinto shrines.

Many of those involved in such campaigns have been members of the Liberal Democratic Party, which despite its name is a conservative movement that has been the main party of government in Japan for most of the time since the mid-1950s. Many of those who want to restore state–religion links and state sponsorship of religion, also would like to restore the Emperor to a position not of constitutional monarch, as now, but to something more exalted, which would hark back to the divine status outlined in Shinto myths.

Yasukuni shrine has featured prominently in these campaigns, partially because it enshrines the spirits of those who died in the war, and perhaps more because it is a potent symbol of the links between state, religion, and the Emperor. It was established in 1869 as a shrine for the spirits of those who died in the fighting that accompanied the Meiji Restoration, and who were as such considered by the new government to be national heroes who had given their lives for the Emperor. Since that time, the spirits of those who have died on behalf of the country have been enshrined at Yasukuni through rituals which transformed their spirits into *kami* and guardian deities of the nation.

Those who died fighting for the Japanese cause in the Second World War are also among those who have been enshrined at Yasukuni; in all around 2.5 million spirits are enshrined there as *kami*. Prior to the war Yasukuni was one of the most important shrines of the state religion, and was supported financially by the state – support that was lost after the separation of religon and state.

Political Manoeuvres and Opposition

Since that time, numerous attempts have been made to provide state funding for the Yasukuni shrine, and a number of bills have been introduced into the Japanese parliament (Diet) by politicians to this end. All have failed to achieve their purpose and have met strong opposition, especially from other religious movements and left-of-centre and liberal politicians.

Those who advocate providing state support for Yasukuni argue that it is, in effect, a war memorial and that, since other countries have their national memorials for the war dead that are supported by the state, Yasukuni should be treated in the same way. They also argue that the Japanese custom of memorializing the dead and paying respects to those who have died in the service of others is a cultural custom, rather than a religious activity, and that therefore providing funds for Yasukuni would not mean breaching the prohibition of state-funding for religious purposes.

The opposition to such attempts is well aware that such claims are disingenuous, designed to get around the laws regulating state and religion. In particular, they fear that any move to fund Yasukuni as a national war memorial would open the way to further attempts to promote Shinto, and lead to the resurgence of militant nationalism, as well as to the renewed links between state and Shinto. The issue has been made more acute by the revelation that in 1978 the Yasukuni shrine also incorporated into its pantheon the spirits of a number of those who had been executed after the war as war criminals.

The enshrinement of those who were associated with the darkest sides of Japanese militarism and nationalism appeared to confirm the concerns of those from Buddhist organizations, new religions and Christian churches to political groupings, ranging from the Japanese Communist Party to many liberal groups, who felt that a dangerous nationalist agenda was in operation.

This feeling was further enhanced on 15 August (the date of the Japan's surrender, and the national day of remembrance for the dead) 1985, when the then Prime Minister, Nakasone Yasuhiro (himself an ardent right-wing nationalist), visited Yasukuni shrine in a formal capacity. This visit raised concerns that Nakasone would throw his weight behind attempts to introduce state patronage of the shrine, which in turn would open the way for a revival of Shinto nationalism and a possible attempt to revise the constitution.

Protests came not only from inside Japan but from many of Japan's neighbours who had suffered the brunt of Japan's nationalist aggression in the pre-war era, and who also felt offended by the apparent spectacle of a Japanese Prime Minister worshipping in an official capacity at a place that enshrined the spirits of executed war criminals. All attempts to change the status of Yasukuni shrine, to provide it with public funds or to interpret what occurs there as custom, have so far failed.

The Yasukuni shrine issue is not the only contentious one relating to Shinto–state affairs, for numerous court cases have been waged over this question in postwar Japan. In one such case, citizens in the town of Tsu in Mie prefecture went to court after the town's mayor had paid local Shinto priests to perform a *jichinsai*, or ground-breaking purification ceremony, prior to the building of a city gymnasium, arguing that the use of public funds in this case for a religious service violated the constitution. The case went as far as the Supreme Court, which eventually ruled that the mayor had not transgressed the law in this case, since *jichinsai* rites are performed so often and widely that people had ceased to be aware of any religious significance to them. Hence the ritual had become secularized and was no longer religious.

The Tsu case was the first one concerned with the question of the separation of religion and state to reach Japan's Supreme Court, and hence its ruling was highly important, seeming to set a precedent and opening the door to some use of state funds in connection with some Shinto rituals. However, in a more recent case a Supreme Court ruling has reaffirmed the separation of state and religion, and ruled against the use of public funds, even in such 'customary' ways. Nevertheless, the picture remains unclear and highly contentious.

In all of this the Yasukuni shrine issue remains the most controversial and critical of all cases, because it is so deeply linked to issues of war and Emperor veneration, and because in enshrining the war dead it appears to glorify the sacrifice of the lives of citizens on behalf of the state. The shrine remains a potent symbol for Shinto religious nationalists and supporters, and is a symbolic reminder to others of the controversies and dangers that have in the past been associated with Shinto in its nationalist manifestations.

Because Yasukuni enshrines the spirits of war criminals too, it is also a reminder of the darker and more problematic aspects of Shinto as a religious tradition that has been used and manipulated by the state and that assisted the cause of militarism, and of the dangers that any revival of the pre-war elements of state Shinto might harbour.

Chapter 8

Shinto in the Modern World

The term Shinto, as we have seen in this guide, encompasses a number of different forms and levels, and is related to controversial elements in Japan's past which continue to cause contention, such as the deification of the Emperor and Japanese militant nationalism. Equally, though, it relates to less controversial themes, from festivals and popular prayer rituals, to simple acts of worship and participation in individual life-cycle and community calendrical ritual occasions, that may be engaged in by Japanese in all walks of life without necessarily implying any inherent religious commitment.

While in everyday terms, the types of Shinto the visitor to Japan is likely to encounter will be of the colourful nature of festivals and shrine visits, the roots and associations of Shinto with Japanese national myths and identity, and the ways these have been manifest in the past, should also be remembered.

However, the problematic issues raised by Shinto's links to nationalism should not be allowed to obscure its deep roots in Japan's history, its roles in the development of Japanese culture, and its interactions with Buddhism which have been at the very foundation of Japanese religious culture.

In considering Shinto's past and present some considerations also need to be given to its future for, despite its position as a Japanese tradition with deep cultural and historical roots, and despite the wide-spread participation of Japanese people in its rituals and festive events, Shinto in the present day is, like other mainstream and established religious traditions, facing uncertain times. This is partly due to changing social, economic and demographic circumstances, partly to the challenges it is facing from other, newer and often more vibrant religious movements, and partly because in the modern age many people are turning their backs on religious activities of all sorts.

Partly it is also due to the fact that Shinto has not travelled overseas with any success or built a community of followers outside Japan: even among the immigrant Japanese communities that were established in places such as Hawaii in the nineteenth and early twentieth centuries, Shinto shrines have hardly flourished. In Hawaii, for instance, as the Japanese community has adapted to the Hawaiian–American cultural sphere, it has paid less and less attention to institutions that are related to a past ethnic identity. While other, more adaptable

Japanese religious institutions such as Buddhist temples and new religions, have maintained their support or grown, Shinto shrines have become run down and lack support, and the new generations of Japanese-Americans feel little empathy with a tradition so closely associated with a land that they do not live in or belong to. Similar pictures can be found elsewhere in Japanese overseas communities.

An Uneven Picture

It is in the Japanese setting that Shinto's future is based, and here the picture is at best mixed. Attendance at major Shinto shrines during mass occasions, such as the New Year festival, has gone up over the past decades and remains high in the present, and such large, nationally known shrines as Meiji Shrine and Fushimi Inari are visited by people from far and wide. At events such as *shichigosan* large crowds throng important and local shrines alike, while shrines catering for benefits and providing a means of assistance in areas such as education receive vast numbers of visitors, especially in the period leading up to school and university entrance examinations.

Shrines such as Ise and Izumo attract enormous hordes of visitors, who often combine a mixture of tourism and pilgrimage in their visits. In all these areas cardinal ideas relating to the nature of Shinto as expressed through its shrines – such as the intermingling of entertainment and prayer, the expression of cyclicality, the expression of belonging and identity, and the belief that the gods are there to help humans in their lives – are manifest. Taken together they present a picture of Shinto as a religious tradition with a thriving modern face, with its bases in ritual expression and participation in events that are associated with life and celebration.

This picture of Shinto, however, is a partial one, for there are also problem areas as well. Politically, as has been seen, Shinto remains ambivalent and problematic, its associations with militarism, right-wing politics and nationalism making it suspect in the eyes of many Japanese as well as outsiders. As a result, several religious organizations in Japan regard Shinto, even at local levels, with some suspicion, to the extent that even seemingly formal ritual functions such as Shinto priests performing dedication services at municipal buildings remain potentially divisive and politically contentious issues.

The attempts by rightist and nationalist politicians to secure funding and support for the Yasukuni shrine occasionally provoke trouble, and have so far consistently failed in their aims, while the efforts of the Jinja Honchō and other Shinto groups to assert the values of Shinto as a national religious tradition remain fraught with potential areas of dispute.

The large national shrines that appear to flourish and attract enormous numbers of visitors have been aided in this by a number of factors related less to religious dynamics than to changing social and economic circumstances. Improved transportation facilities have made it more feasible to travel further to visit shrines, and this, linked to the sense of national sentiment fostered by the mass media at times such as New Year, helps to stimulate visits to the well-known shrines.

This pattern of prosperity does not always, however, filter down to smaller or more regional shrines. A combination of rural depopulation and greater mobility has eroded the support bases of regional and local shrines, many of which are unable to support a priest.

Changing demographic patterns and changes in the social patterns of households (most particularly the growth of nuclear rather than extended households, and the growing tendency to single-person households) have also undermined the household–community shrine relationships upon which local Shinto shrines relied.

Rise and Challenge of New Religions

In the changing religious and cultural world of late twentieth-century Japan, with its rapid changes, its increasing urbanization and the growth of individualism, older traditions such as Shinto (and indeed Buddhism) often appeared out of touch with the contemporary mood, and vulnerable to challenges from newer and more dynamic religious forces. The emergence of new religious movements, a feature of the Japanese religious landscape since the mid-nineteenth century, has cut deeply into the support structures of Shinto and Buddhism and drawn followers away from them.

Many of the new religions draw their main themes and ideas from Buddhist, Shinto and folk religious sources, but reinterpret them in ways relevant and appealing to people in the context of changing historical circumstances. Thus, for example, many of the early new religions emerged in the mid-nineteenth century in rural Japan, in part in response to the rapid social and economic changes of the times – changes that the older, established religious traditions appeared unable to cope with.

Many of these early new religions, such as Tenrikyō and Kurozumikyō, were influenced by Shinto and assumed Shinto-style ritual forms, and were, indeed, for a period in the earlier part of the century officially classified as 'sectarian Shinto' movements. Later, new religions, some with a Shinto basis, some Buddhist, and others a mixture of a variety of religious influences, have continued to develop and grow in Japan. These represent both a challenge to, and to some extent a criticism of, Shinto and of Buddhism.

One of the main reasons why such movements have developed and have attracted ardent and large active worship followings, is because of the failures of the older religions to fulfil the spiritual needs of large sections of the populace at any deeper level than that of the social patterns of religion and of the ritual and calendrical cycles.

This situation was particularly acute in the immediate post-war years in Japan, when Shinto was discredited because of its wartime associations, and in this era the new religions grew and proliferated at an extraordinary rate, providing spiritual solace for the Japanese people in ways that Shinto at the time appeared incapable of, and helping them to deal with the shocks of defeat, occupation and impoverishment.

In the 1990s, new waves of new religions attracted younger people in urban settings, and further eroded the support base of the older religions. While Shinto and Buddhism continue to receive loyal support due to their roles in the ritual household and life-cycle processes, and from the older generations, they cannot depend solely on these in the future and need to replace these supporters as they die out. Indeed, they face the problem of attracting the support of the younger generation who, while they may occasionally attend a shrine before their examinations, may be less interested in many of the ritual aspects of Shinto and of religion in general, who may not have their parents' sense of deference for and adherence to older customs, or who may be more interested in the new religions than in older traditions.

An Unclear Future

All in all, then, the future looks unclear for Shinto. At some levels as a tradition based on the interactions of often casual and pragmatic levels between Japanese people and *kami*, it remains vibrant, yet it displays underlying weaknesses, from its decaying rural and wayside shrines, to the potentially divisive aspects of its political past.

Shinto's position as a religion without strong doctrinal bases and associated with a particular place and set of meanings and identities gives it the flexibility to adapt to changing situations and economic patterns. Its deities, such as Inari, are able to appeal to different communities at different times, as with Inari's role as a rice deity, relevant to a rural community, and as a god of business for modern firms.

However, despite such flexibility and despite the crowds drawn in by its pageantry and its close associations with events and entertainments, it also is faced with the possibility of ending up as little more than a colourful, if evocative, symbol of Japanese tradition and customs – attracting crowds to its biggest shrines at special occasions, yet lacking any core meanings capable of appealing to, and fulfilling the needs of, people in today's rapidly changing cultural climate. Equally, while there are voices calling for renewed state support for the tradition, such advocates are often more closely identified with the vestiges of the past than with the promises of the future.

Operating most actively in the present day at localized, practical and festive levels, and with close associations with the celebration and enhancement of life in Japan, Shinto is also encumbered by the spectres of its recent past, and its support structures eroded by the changing nature and needs of contemporary Japanese society. How far it will be able to cope with such changes and remain relevant is as yet uncertain.

The importance of its role in the development of Japanese religious culture so far, however, is not in doubt, for Shinto has been central to the formation of Japanese religious culture, providing it and the Japanese people with a series of myths and religious concepts and a virtually infinite array of figures of worship – the *kami* – at its core, which cater to the needs of the Japanese people and are the focus of the rituals and festivals through which much of the dynamism of Shinto may be seen today.

Glossary

Buddha Buddhist term referring to (1) the founder of the Buddhist religion and (2) to other figures of worship in the Buddhist pantheon who have attained enlightenment. In Japan, the term 'buddha' (hotoke, butsu) is widely used to refer to figures of worship at Buddhist temples. See also shinbutsu.

Ema votive tablet, usually made of wood (see Chapter Six).

Enmusubi joining people together in love or marriage: a popular attribute of kami, and a benefit that many people pray for.

Fuda talisman, symbolising the presence of the kami, it has either protective functions, warding off bad luck, or beckoning ones, bringing good luck (see Chapter Six).

Gūji chief priest of a Shinto shrine.

Hatsumōde the first shrine visit of the year: refers to the New Year's festival and the custom of making a visit to a shrine at this time.

Harai (alternatively *harae*) purification ritual.

Hatsumiyamairi first shrine visit, when a baby is taken, usually within thirty days of birth, to the shrine by parents and grandparents to be placed under the protection of the *kami* and receive their blessing.

Hitogami *kami* believed to have derived from humans.

Honden main hall of worship at a shrine where the spirit of the *kami* is believed to reside.

Hotoke alternative reading of the ideogram *butsu* (buddha): in Japan this may refer to a spirit of the dead or a buddha.

Hyakudo mairi 'hundred times around' – the practice of circumambulating two stones, usually placed in a shrine courtyard, in order to acquire merit and make supplications to the *kami* to help one.

Jichinsai ground breaking ceremony: a standard ritual ceremony conducted when a new building is constructed or dedicated, carried out by a Shinto priest who involves the local *kami*, asks their protection and enshrines them as protectors of the building.

Jingū important shrine

Jinja shrine

Kami Shinto deity (see Chapter Two)

Kannushi standard term for a Shinto priest

Kojiki important text produced in the eighth century as a mythical outline of Japan's origins and of its founding by the *kami*.

Miko shrine maiden: ritual officiant who works at a shrine, serving, for example, as an intermediary in rituals (see Chapters Four and Five).

Mikoshi portable shrine in which *kami* are temporarily enshrined and carried in procession during festivals

Nenjū gyōji yearly rituals/events: the term refers to the cycle of annual ritual events in a shrine's or temple's calendar.

Nihon Shoki (Nihongi) text written roughly at the same time as the *Kojiki*, with a slightly more historical angle to it, purporting to outline the deeds and lineages of Japan's Imperial rulers.

Norito Shinto prayers used in rituals to venerate the *kami* and address the wishes of the faithful to them. The tenth-century text the *Engi-Shiki* contains some of the earliest examples of such prayers, but new *norito* (generally using archaic terminology) continue to be created for new needs and prayer rituals.

(O)mamori protective amulet usually worn on the person to ward off danger or bring good luck.

Matsuri festival (see Chapter Five).

Sakaki sacred tree, whose branches are used in numerous Shinto rituals; for example, a sprig of *sakaki* may be waved over the heads of participants during purification blessings, to symbolically wipe away spiritual impurities, or it may be carried during Shinto processions, as a symbol of life.

Shichigosan means 'seven–five–three' and refers to the annual festival in November (usually 15 November) when girls aged seven and three, and boys aged five are taken to the shrine for a blessing and to renew their protection by the *kami*.

Shimenawa straw rope from which usually strips of paper, cloth or straw, are hung: it designates the presence of the *kami* and of sacred locations.

Shinbutsu this term combines the ideograms for *kami* (shin) and *hotoke* (butsu), and is used to refer jointly to the figures of worship found at Shinto shrines and Buddhist temples that are prayed to for worldly benefits, grace and help.

Shintai 'body of the *kami*' – an object which is believed to house the spirit of a *kami* and which is kept in the inner sanctum of the shrine.

Shinwa myth: the word literally means a 'tale of the *kami*'.

Suzu cluster of bells which are used as a ritual implement of purification.

Taisha 'great shrine': title of important shrines such as Izumo Taisha.

Temizuya 'hand washing place': fountain or water source at the entrance to shrines, where worshippers can purify themselves by washing their hands and mouths out.

Torii Shinto gateway through which one passes to enter the shrine: usually two slanting pillars with two crosspieces, made of wood and painted vermillion, although many contemporary ones are concrete and occasionally metal.

Ujigami clan or community deities (*kami*); they may be the spirits of clan ancestors venerated for having given life to the clan, but are commonly, in the present day, the *kami* of local communities or villages.

Ujiko 'child of the clan' – term referring to parishioners of a shrine, members of a household which is in the district of a shrine and has obligations (in terms of participation in shrine events, and payments of dues) to support the shrine.

Yakudoshi 'unlucky year' – times in the life-cycle (chiefly the 33rd year for women and 42nd for men) which are considered unlucky and in which the *kami*'s protection is especially needed: it is common for people to make special shrine visits and perform special rituals at this time.

Further Reading

Michael Ashkenazi. *Matsuri*. University of Hawaii Press, Honolulu, 1993.

Brian Bocking. *A Popular Dictionary of Shinto*. Curzon Press, London, 1996.

Reiko Mochinaga Brandon and Barbara Stephan, with Sumiko Enbutsu and Ian Reader *Spirit and Symbol: The Japanese New Year*. Honolulu Academy of Arts, Honolulu, USA, 1994.

Jan van Bremen and D. P. Martinez (eds.) *Ceremony and Ritual in Japan: Religious Practices in an Industrialized Society*. Routledge, London, 1995. (Contains several chapters on or relating to Shinto, Shinto rituals and shrines.)

Helen Hardacre. *Shinto and the State 1868–1988*. Princeton University Press, Princeton, USA.

Japanese Religion: A Survey by the Agency for Cultural Affairs. Kodansha, Tokyo, 1972. (Contains a chapter on Shinto, plus general information on religion in Japan.)

Mark R. Mullins, Susumu Shimazono and Paul L. Swanson (eds.) *Religion and Society in Modern Japan*. Asian Humanities Press, Berkeley, California, USA, 1993. (Especially pp. 75–132 on Religion and the State.)

John K. Nelson. *A Year in the Life of a Shinto Shrine*. University of Washington Press, Seattle, USA, 1996.

Sokyo Ono. *Shinto: the Kami Way*. Charles Tuttle, Tokyo, 1995. (Original edition 1962.)

Ian Reader. *Religion in Contemporary Japan*. Macmillan and University of Hawaii Press: Basingstoke, UK, and Honolulu, USA, 1991.

Ian Reader, Esben Andreasen and Finn Stefansson. *Japanese Religions Past and Present*. Japan Library, Sandgate, UK, 1994.

Ian Reader and George J. Tanabe Jr. *Practically Religious: Worldly Benefits and the Common Religion of Japan*. University of Hawaii Press, Honolulu, USA, 1998.

Karen A. Smyers. *The Fox and the Jewel: Inari Worship in Contemporary Japan*. University of Hawaii Press, Honolulu, USA, 1998.

Index